THE POLITICAL ECONOMY
OF SAUDI ARABIA

NEAR EASTERN STUDIES
University of Washington
Number 1

This book was published with
the assistance of a grant from
Gull Industries Incorporated of
Seattle, Washington

the Political Economy of Saudi Arabia

A. Reza S. Islami
Rostam Mehraban Kavoussi

Distributed by
UNIVERSITY OF WASHINGTON PRESS
Seattle and London

Sponsored by
The Department of
Near Eastern Languages and Civilization
and
The Henry M. Jackson
School of International Studies
University of Washington

Distributed by
UNIVERSITY OF WASHINGTON PRESS
Seattle and London

Contents

List of Tables

Acknowledgments

The launching of the Near Eastern Studies series at the University of Washington would not have been possible without the enthusiasm and indefatigable endeavors of Jere L. Bacharach, Director of the Middle East Center; the valuable help of Nicholas L. Heer, Chairman of the Department of Near Eastern Languages and Literature; the initial fund raising efforts of Farhat J. Ziadeh, former Director of the Middle East Center and Chairman of the Department of Near Eastern Languages and Literature; indispensible contributions of Pierre A. MacKay, Professor of Classics and Near Eastern Languages and Literature; and the support of the Henry M. Jackson School of International Studies.

Many Saudi citizens gave much time, provided countless insights into the workings of the Saudi Arabian system, brought obscure but important sources to the attention of the authors, and checked the translations of Arabic sources. The authors are very much indebted to them; but knowing that they wish to remain anonymous, we do not name them. However, they will recognize their contributions throughout the manuscript.

Several individuals read and commented on the manuscript at its various stages of development. In particular we would like to thank Joel S. Migdal of the University of Washington, and Djavad Salehi Isfahani of the University of Pennsylvania. We are also grateful to Felicia J. Hecker, Director of Near Eastern Publications at the University of Washington, for overseeing the project.

We would like to thank Susan Steinmann, formerly the Director of Development for the Jackson School, who helped secure initial funding for the project; Garry Davis, our research assistant for the Saudi project, who performed above and beyond the call of duty; and Norine Weston and Elaine DuRall, who typed the original manuscript and its revisions.

The financial contribution of Gull Industries of Seattle and other corporations is greatly appreciated.

Many individuals and institutions have generously contributed to this work. However, the responsibility for its content and the perspective within which the research is presented lies with the authors alone.

Introduction

In much of the literature on Middle Eastern politics, Saudi Arabia is portrayed as having a stable political system and patrimonial form of government that agrees with its deeply traditional social and cultural mores. Furthermore, it is argued that this functional equilibrium between the state and society is supported by oil riches. The country's meager population, it is presumed, will remain content, given the vast financial resources of the state. The various forms of mobilization of support, such as access to policy makers in the form of weekly sittings, *mujalis*, and informal consultations in ad hoc committees, know as *shaur*, are at times considered sufficient to make Saudi Arabia a "desert democracy." The smooth process of succession in 1975 upon King Faisal's assassination, and the peaceful transfer of the throne to King Fahd after King Khalid's death in 1982 are taken as indicators of the system's stability.

The Library of Congress system of Arabic transliteration, without the diacritical marks, is used throughout this manuscript. Exceptions are a few personal names, which follow their owner's preferred transliteration, and commonly anglicized terms.

The kingdom, in fact, has been one of the more stable countries in the Middle East. The process of political succession has generally been orderly. And the boom brought about by oil exports has transformed the lives of many Saudis from poverty to prosperity. However, in the case of Saudi Arabia it is wrong to project the present into the future, and hence presume historical continuity. Saudi Arabia, as a society, is not frozen in time. But the Saudi state on the other hand, shows little indication of an ability to adapt.

The state that was established by 'Abd al-'Aziz (d. 1953), the able founder of the present dynasty, was rooted in a fragmentary society. During the opening years of this century various solipsistic economies and societies existed side by side in the Arabian peninsula. This atomized social structure was unable to offer sustained resistance to the dynastic ambitions of the Saudi family. The destruction of the Ottoman Empire and the concomitant supremacy of the British in the Middle East provided the external framework within which 'Abd al-'Aziz built his state. However, the new monarch failed to effect lasting institutions. Even the famed Brotherhoods, al-Ikhwan, developed independently and were eventually crushed by the king. The Saudi rule, in the final analysis, was made possible through the dynamics of internal opposition that existed among the various parts of this segmentary society and the dependent relationship between the royal family and the British government.

In the past fifty years, two major developments have taken place. First, the United States has replaced Britain. The Saudi dependent relation with the United States is far more complex and sophisticated than the simple political support it received from Britain. Second, as a result of the expansion of oil exports, a more monumental change, namely, the political, social, and economic integration of the Saudi society has taken place. The economy, organized around production and export of oil, has become unified. The differences among tribes and clans are replaced by differences in income and access to the central authority. The erosion of localistic, atavistic, and primordial bonds has increasingly led to the development of a nation with an embryonic modern class structure. The rapid growth of the oil revenues has thus caused major changes in Saudi Arabia's economy and society, and has set the stage for a period of considerable political tension within the kingdom. The non-oil production and labor force have both shifted toward construction and services, and the economy's dependence on imported goods and manpower has increased dramatically. The class structure has changed accordingly, and it is expected to undergo further transformation in the next twenty years. The population has shifted toward major urban areas, and the process of politicization and rising expectations are well under way. Because of its massive oil income, the government has become the most important economic force in the kingdom, and its actions have significant impact on the allocation of resources and the distribution of income.

In spite of fundamental changes in the economy and society, the government of Saudi Arabia has remained in an embryonic stage of development. Above all, the Saudi state is a family matter. While this was in congruence with the segmentary society, its survival in a national epoch is in doubt. The cycles of intensive oil production necessitated by the demand of the industrial economies, and vast monetary outlays as a consequence of inflated revenues, require and bring about a social structure consisting of bureaucrats, technicians, and an urban work force whose interest, political or economic, may differ from those of the patrimonial state. Co-optation, so far, has kept potential opponents in check. But extensive co-optation, which is required, given the advent of urbanization and mass education, will inevitably affect the system's cohesion.

The Saudi system is not ready to face the coming crisis. It has failed to build viable institutions. Its bureaucracy is fundamentally a patronage system. Its military is not only small, but is intentionally fragmented. The old pillars of the system are also eroding fast. The piety of the ruling family is increasingly considered hypocritical. The *majalis* are no longer occasions for the rulers to gain a feel for the populace, but have deteriorated into audiences where suppliants present their requests for financial assistance. Nor is the succession process going to work smoothly. While it has been possible for the sons of the founder to agree among themselves, in the future such agreements among the many grandchildren of 'Abd al-'Aziz will be more difficult to reach. One may anticipate that the crisis of political succession will ignite the more deeply rooted conflict between the state and the society.

This study is largely an attempt to analyze the forces that are transforming the Saudi society and to assess how socioeconomic change may affect the stability of the present political system. Chapter one traces the development of the Saudi state and reviews the historical legacies that are still affecting the Saudi polity. The contemporary political institutions that support the state are analyzed in chapter two. Chapter three examines the sources of economic growth in Saudi Arabia and discusses the impact of oil revenues upon the structure of the economy and labor force. In chapter four the economic forces that are transforming the Saudi society are reviewed and an attempt is made to forecast the class structure that is likely to emerge in the kingdom. Chapter five discusses the economic role of the state and presents a preliminary investigation of the manner in which oil revenues and government policy have affected the pattern of income distribution; and finally chapter six studies the roots and the manifestations of political opposition in the kingdom.

THE POLITICAL ECONOMY
OF SAUDI ARABIA

1

The Development
of the Saudi State

A SEGMENTED SOCIETY

Until the emergence of the Saudi family as the predominant force in the 1920s, Arabia was a society in stalemate.[1] The society, which was mostly nomadic, was divided into tribes that kept each other in check; and each tribe was in turn divided into many tribal subdivisions. Expansion of the power of any one tribe brought about the alliance of others in opposition to it. Conflicts were over real issues such as pasture land and water rights. Ritualistic conflicts and wars over ideologies were uncommon in Arabia. Disputes, therefore, could be readily resolved and they often were.

Absolute right and wrong did not exist. Justice, *'adl* in Arabic, refers to establishing an equilibrium between the two sides of the saddle bag. Indeed, *'adl* in Arabia was a state of reasonable compromise between two sides in such a way that neither was irreparably harmed. The concept was, therefore, more associated with a balancing process than justice. The society consequently faced continuous tension, but the tension was not allowed to grow out of bounds. The nature of conflicts and mechanism of its resolution were such that the system remained stable for over a millenium.

Unlike European cities, which brought about social change, Arabian cities were too few, too far from each other, and too insecure against tribal incursions to alter the course of Arabian history. Originally settled by nomads, these cities not only manifested the cultural mores of the tribe, but they acted to maximize their interests within a fundamentally tribal social structure. They became centers of exchange and trade but not manufacturing.

The political insecurity of the urban areas and the nomadic social structure retarded social and economic development by making individual property holding meaningless, limiting markets, and lowering the level of capital formation. The meager economy did not support a complex class structure, the inner conflict of which might have transformed the society from one historical stage to the next. The degree of exchange was limited; the amount of economic surplus was small; and the difference between the rich and poor was slight. Personal conflicts, tribal feuds, raids, and banditry conceal the fact that Arabia was, historically speaking, stagnant. Personal changes did not signify systematic changes. Men fished, dived for pearls, herded camels, and traded handicrafts as they had for a millenium. The sheik held the tribal *majlis*, where members of the community presented their ideas and the sheik made decisions, combining personalism and customs. There was little societal integration. There was, in fact, no single identifiable society, politically, socially, or economically.[2]

THE FORMATION OF THE SAUDI STATE

The Saudi state is closely associated with the ideology propagated by Muhammad Ibn 'Abd al-Wahhab in the

1740s. Teaching a fundamental return to the purity and simplicity of Islam of earlier days, he was found too dangerous in his hometown. Expelled from home, he sought refuge in Dariya, then ruled by Amir Muhammad Ibn Sa'ud, an ancestor of the present ruling family. Conversion to the new faith infused Amir Muhammad with a sense of mission. The level of conflict was raised from real to ideal, from local to systemic. Ibn 'Abd al-Wahhab's teachings formed a new ideology that underpinned the development of a state beyond the horizon of one tribe. This ideology became the basis for a unity that had not existed earlier. Before his death in 1765, Amir Muhammad and his converted nomads brought Nejd (eastern Arabia), under their control. His successors, building on the same religious enthusiasm, conquered almost all of Arabia and parts of Syria and Iraq. The Ottoman Empire, a major threat to Saudi regional and independent power, brought the Saudi's first triumphs to an end. Directed by the Ottomans, the army of Muhammad 'Ali, the viceroy of Egypt, began the reconquest of Arabia in 1814 and finally expelled the Saudis from their traditional seat of power, Dariya, in 1820. The first Saudi state came to an end and the family took refuge in Kuwait.

Had the Saudis been just another ruling Arab family, exile in Kuwait would have marked their end. Although their political power was diminished, the Saudis still laid claim to the rulership. Their ideological position had helped to convert many Arabs into a new religious zeal. Muhammad Ibn 'Abd al-Wahhab, it is presumed, had transferred his position as the imam, religious leader, to the Saud family. It was this dual political and religious power that helped the family to strike out again. The deterioration of the Ottoman Empire as a regional power and the deeper penetration of the Middle East by imperial forces also facilitated the second emergence of the family.

In 1902, 'Abd al-'Aziz Ibn Sa'ud moved to recapture
Arabia with, as tradition would have it, barely forty men
on horseback. The British, who were interested in under-
mining the Ottomans, supplied him with limited financial
support and even more limited technical support. Pro–
Ottoman sheiks fell to the Saudis, and Riyadh was cap-
tured in 1902. In 1927, 'Abd al-'Aziz was declared the king
of Hejaz (the western region) and Nejd. By 1930 the borders of contemporary Saudi Arabia were carved and in
1932 the newly formed country was named after the family,
the Kingdom of Saudi Arabia.[3]

EARLY BASES OF SUPPORT

Foreign Support

As early as 1915, 'Abd al-'Aziz was accompanied and advised by a British officer, Captain W. Shakespear. By the
end of 1915, 'Abd al-'Aziz's rule over Nejd, Hasa, Jubail,
and Qatif was recognized and guaranteed by the British
in a formal treaty. At that time, Britain was the major
imperial force in the Persian Gulf area. The British recog-
nition of 'Abd al-'Aziz's authority was not merely a formal-
ity; it was a signal to other power groups to accept his
suzerainty. The British, in fact, guaranteed the integrity
of the kingdom, which 'Abd al-'Aziz was busy creating. A
£5,000 subsidy, machine guns, and rifles sent from Britain
were instrumental in the formation of the Saudi kingdom.[4]

Religious Support

What distinguished 'Abd al-'Aziz's claim to power from
other tribal sheiks was his supratribal authority based on
the new faith. It was a unifying factor, which was to become a new basis of authority and solidarity. Tribe after tribe submitted to 'Abd al-'Aziz. Tribal leaders became
bound to him not only through alliance but through con-

version into the new faith. The existing segmental society of Arabia, whose parts maintained unity through balanced opposition and tension and whose unity could be negatively defined, was transformed into a society that was united through ideology. The members of this new society had developed an exclusive identity based on Wahhabism, which clearly aligned them against nonbelievers. This religiously based solidarity generated support for the king, who had assumed the religious title of imam.[5]

Islam had, of course, existed in Arabia for centuries. But as it was practiced, it was too communal and mystical to become a guide for social action on a systemic level. Tribal mores, tradition, and structure were all presumed to be an aspect of the divine. God and men mingled together. The Wahhabi emphasis of God's absoluteness, distance, and his unforgiving nature, like Weberian analysis of Protestantism, sanctioned the development of a new spirit. Through acceptance of a higher form of authority, placed outside the individual and tribal association, a unified society became possible.

It is generally accepted as a truism that Wahhabism under the leadership of 'Abd al-'Aziz developed an organizational format in religious military associations known as Ikhwan. It is further assumed that the Ikhwan movement cut across tribal associations and became the military organization that put the Saudi family in power. The discussion is not of historical interest alone for it throws light on the ability of the new system to build institutions and thus permit a stable government.

Further research, however, indicates that the Ikhwan organization was created by 'Abd al-Karim al-Muqrabi, a theology teacher from Iraq, independent of the Saudi family. In fact, 'Abd al-'Aziz was alarmed to find out of its existence and was advised by his influential cousin, 'Abd Allah Jiluwi, governor of Ahsa, to end the movement before it could gain power. After vacillating for some time, 'Abd al-'Aziz finally decided to lend support to the movement and make it his own.[6] That the Ikhwan movement became antagonistic toward the Saudis almost from the beginning and that they felt the need for suppressing it at its infancy, supports the contention outlined above. Seventeen years after the creation of the movement, the Saud family fought the Ikhwan and defeated it in 1930. Within a short time the movement ended.[7]

The Ikhwan, contrary to most writings on Saudi Arabia, was not a success. Not only was it short-lived but it did not accomplish what it set out to do. Ikhwan settlements were few and those that existed retained their tribal structures. They did not become agricultural communities of religious believers loyal to the Saudis. Leadership of each Ikhwan settlement remained in the hands of the tribal sheik.[8] Consequently, it did not and could not replace the tribe as a social organization.

Religion, in a diffuse form, lent support to the Saudis. However, the Saudis were unable to transform this support into a social structure. The bulk of writings on Saudi Arabia consider the Ikhwan a lasting institutional achievement. Closer scrutiny shows that it was neither a Saudi creation nor an enduring institution. This failure to build institutions in the formative years of the regime is indicative of the inherent weakness of the system. Diffuse support, while essential for stability, is not sufficient. In the face of crises, the stability of a system hinges on institutional support. The state that was formed by the Saudis was institutionally weak from the beginning.

EMERGENCE OF PATRIMONIAL KINGSHIP

The final defeat of the Ikhwan movement in 1930 marks the beginning of the Saudi state. The Saudi family used violent means to gain control and no other group could prove a realistic threat to them. The basis of support for the Saudis shifted from the tribesmen of Nejd to the urbanites of Hejaz. It was with the support of the latter group that the Ikhwan movement was crushed. It is also the latter group that to this day continues to fill the major bureaucratic positions. The tribes have lost much of their importance. By and large they have become settled in towns. Nevertheless, they still manifest some tribal mores and structures within cities. As a military threat, they have lost their significance, given the predominance of the money economy, the creation of a standing army, as well as importation of modern means of warfare. The Saudis rule independent of tribes. The tribes, on the other hand, are dependent on the state for subsidies. Nor are the subsidies from the traditional sources. Oil income has pushed both traditional economy and power centers into the periphery. The monarch is no longer a sheik among other sheiks. No longer does he have to make alliances and compromises with other tribal leaders. Increasingly, he has become a monarch more like the absolutist European kings than those who ruled earlier in Arabia through segmental opposition.

In fact, the power of the Saudi ruler is more extensive than the European absolutist monarch. He is not dependent on the bourgeoisie's tax money. His revenue comes from oil, which is practically considered to be his. Various classes of his subjects depend on him and the mode of distribution of funds he chooses. The so-called desert democracy has no reality here anymore. The sheiks of tribes no longer sit in a *majlis*, the traditional consultative assembly. They have little place in a society in which the grand sheik has become the monarch, the commander in chief, the prime minister, the religious head, the highest tribal authority, and the dispenser of social status and economic rewards.

The state has become autonomous; its claims to power are independent of traditional forces with the partial exception of the religious structure and the National Guard. In the process it has become increasingly dependent on foreign support, namely the United States, and an embryonic modern, urban, class structure. The middle class, who fill the technical positions, are becoming vital to the survival of the state as is the working class, which is foreign to a large extent. The internal pillars of the system presently are the military, the religious structure, and the bureaucracy, all of which are extensions of the ruling family.

Contemporary Arabia is an ideal model of a patrimonial system where the realm is conceived to be the property of the ruler. There is only one other state in the world that is named after the ruling family—Hashemite Jordan. In a system such as this, bureaucratic positions are considered pieces of revenue to be distributed among family members and other members of the household. Thus, it is not surprising that the king is also the prime minister; one of his brothers is minister of interior; another is minister of defense whose deputies are his brothers; and a nephew is minister of foreign affairs.

Important governorships are distributed among members of the royal household in the same manner. The governor of the Western Province is Amir Majid, King Fahd's brother. Another brother 'Abd al-Muhsin, is in charge of the administration of the holy city of Medina, and the important governorship of Riyadh is assigned to Salman, King Fahd's most trusted brother. A score of nephews rule over important provinces such as Asir and Hejaz. The Eastern Province has been traditionally governed by the Jiluwi family, a branch of the Saudi family.

Other positions that are less important to the immediate security and that require technical knowledge are entrusted to sons of families who have been traditionally associated with the royal clan. For the most part, they consist of urbanites from Hejaz who serve the family but have no important social base to threaten the family's monopoly of power. Men such as 'Abd al-'Aziz al-Quwaiz, who has the crucial position of certifying contractors, Muhammad 'Ali Aba al-Khail, minister of finance, Hisham Nazir, minister of planning, and Zaki Yamani, minister of oil, come from Hejaz families whose father served the founder of the second Saudi dynasty. Similarly, religious affairs are under the authority of the Shaikh family who were instrumental in bringing religious support to 'Abd al-'Aziz.

The most important contractors and importers are also men whose fathers were trusted advisers to 'Abd al-'Aziz. The Juffali brothers, Ghaith Far'un, and Adhan Khashoggi are the major examples of this category. The senior Juffali, a merchant, was a friend of 'Abd al-'Aziz's who helped finance his campaigns. Khashoggi's father was 'Abd al-'Aziz's physician and confidant, and Far'un is the son of the late King Faisal's closest adviser.

It is a mistake to consider these individuals private capitalists. They exercise the kind of power that is often reserved for governmental agencies. As one observer put it, they are to Saudi government what the Hudson Bay Company was to the British government.[9] Their financial ability is directly related to their contact with the government and their fortunes are derived from government contracts and monopoly rights. The Juffali brothers built the telegraph system for Jidda, brought electricity to Mecca, and act as sales agents for about three hundred companies among which are International Business Machines, Volkswagen, and Siemens. The fortunes of these families are directly related to their monopoly rights as members of the Saudi household. In fact, most economic activities of this group take place in conjunction with royal participation. It is reputed, for example, that Dalla, a monopoly com-

pany that controls such state functions as airport maintenance and city services, is owned by four of the late
King Faisal's sons (Turki, 'Abd Allah, Sa'ud, and Khalid)
together with two commoners from Hejaz: Hisham Nazir,
minister of planning, and Muhammad al-Yamani, minister
of information until his fall from grace in April 1983.

The structural changes brought about by the social
transition from a tribal society into a full-fledged patrimonial kingship based on the control of oil revenues has led to
interesting but not surprising developments. Traditionally,
Arabia was divided into *qabiliun* (tribes), and *khadhiri*
(settled population) mostly in western Saudi Arabia. Socially, the *qabiliun* were placed higher than the *khadhiri*s.
A small group of foreigners existed in religious cities such
as Mecca or in ports such as Jidda. This last group ranked
lowest in social prestige. As a consequence of centralization
of power and subjugation of the value system to money,
the social hierarchy in Arabia has gone through radical
change. Not only is it the Hejazi bureaucrat who is notice-
ably more favorably placed than the tribal chief from Nejd,
but the foreign group has also come to command positions
of influence and prestige. Members of this class include
Kamal Adham, of Turkish origin, who as King Faisal's
brother-in-law headed the intelligence services and now is
the most important arms salesman in Arabia; and Rashad
Far'un, a Syrian who was the chief royal adviser and the
physician to 'Abd al-'Aziz.[10] Khashoggi is another case in
point. One may add the American advisers to this group,
also. The emergence of this group as a wielder of influence
is indicative of the direction of the state. The monarchy
in Arabia now requires men with some technical ability,
who at the same time are not socially powerful enough
to challenge its authority. The fact that these individuals
have become influential is a testimony to the power of the
king as the source from which most power and prestige em-

anates. One should note, however, that the consciousness of superiority of the *qabiliun* is not lost and their resentment of their demotion on the social scale may one day have serious political ramifications.

2

The Structure of Rulership

THE BUREAUCRATIC STRUCTURE

The institutional support for the patrimonial monarch, which has played havoc with Arabian social structure, is very weak. Most bureaucratic positions are of recent origins. The exercise of discretionary authority, marked by personalism at every level, has retarded the growth of institutions. Given the number of persons of royal blood and the thousands of others who are members of the households of the princes, it would be impossible for formal regulations to be enacted and applied uniformly. Without formalization, depersonalization, and regulation no bureaucracy can exist. In Arabia, on the contrary, bureaucratic positions are considered pieces of revenue that legitimately belong to the members of one's household. The office is not separated from the person. The astounding size of the bureaucracy in Arabia is only an indication of thousands who are beneficiaries of government subsidies. Those who actually perform official tasks are too few. The monarchy needs an able and efficient adminstration, but the style, mores, and content of the patrimonial authority rebel against the requirements of a bureaucracy. The bureaucratic positions in this patrimonial kingdom are considered to be primarily a means of livelihood that belongs to the family members. As a result, nearly all important positions are filled by the Saudi royal family. Positions of lesser importance that require some expertise are filled by members of the Saudi household; and at the bottom of the bureaucratic ladder are a large number of hangers-on that must be taken care of. Any rationalization of the bureaucracy will have adverse effects on those who are in positions of bringing about rationalization. Consequently, it is not surprising that good intentions are often expressed but immediately abandoned.

A constitution intended to regularize the form of the government was promised by the late King Faisal upon his accession to the throne. This was not the first or the last time that such a promise was given. At times of crisis, in response to popular demands, the monarch normally declares his wish to codify a body of written rules and establish some sort of national assembly. But once the crisis is over, the attempts to regularize the government are forgotten. Thus the structure of the state is still personal, affairs are handled case by case, allowing for much official discretion. In the absence of rules and regulations, no one's area of jurisdiction is clearly marked. Subject to personalistic and erratic rule from above and unprotected by any written codes or job descriptions, the official tends to postpone decisions or pass them on. The situation is inherently subject to corruption. The safest course for the official is not to make a decision. The system is, therefore, internally immobilized.

The history of bureaucratic structure in Arabia is a recent one. One of the first ministries to be instituted, given the dependent nature of the Saudi regime, was that of foreign affairs. Like other patrimonial offices, it emerged from the household of the king. Prince Faisal, the future monarch, who was his father's contact with the British, was appointed the director of foreign affairs in 1925. In 1930, the Directorate became a ministry. Money was the other important concern to the embryonic regime. Like the Ministry of Foreign Affairs, the Ministry of Finance grew out of the ruler's household in 1933. The first minister of finance, 'Abd Allah Sulaiman al-Hamdan, a household servant of 'Abd al-'Aziz's ran the ministry as if it were the king's private purse. Naturally as the simple tribal system became more complex, new functions should have been assigned to persons who had performed similar functions for the ruler. What is surprising and alarming is that the system has remained frozen since its formative years.

Some of the king's closest advisers were foreigners. For example, Hafiz Wahba, an Egyptian, directed the education system; Yusuf Yasin, a Syrian, was a political secretary to the king; and St. John Philby, a Briton, advised the king on political matters. The dependence on foreign nationals has increased over the years and now nascent nationalistic feelings make such a dependent relationship even more unpalatable. Such dependence often is a result of the unreliability of one's own subjects and the lack of elite-forming institutions or the unwillingness to create them.

Under the impact of oil revenues, new ministries have sprung up but they are still mostly skeletons manned by officials who manifest only a rudimentary understanding of their offices. However, no Council of Ministers existed until 1953 and throughout the fifties it remained an exclusive club of six princes, two advisers to the king, and a merchant from Jidda who did business with and for the royal family. The conflict between King Saud and Crown Prince Faisal in the fifties weakened the solidarity of the family so much that each royal faction tried to strengthen its position by allying itself with nonroyal elements. Thus, the Council of Ministers that was instituted by Saud in

1960 included five nonroyal members. The selection of the new ministers was as much based on their political reliability as it was based on their education. Four of them held degrees from Cairo University and the fifth was a graduate of the University of Texas. The growing complexity of the government necessitated the recruitment of new elements who had an appreciation for the modern world. A conscious effort to ally the regime with the educated and trusted segment of the middle class should not, however, be overlooked. This process was accelerated under King Faisal when nine out of fourteen positions in the council were filled by nonroyal members.[1] The membership of the Council of Ministers was altered again in 1975, during the reign of King Khalid. Including the king himself, who was also the premier, and Crown Prince Fahd, who was officially the first deputy prime minister but in fact was in charge of the council, and Prince Abdallah who was the second deputy prime minister, there were only five other princes in the new council, which had been expanded to twenty-six positions.[2]

Commoners filled many other important bureaucratic positions as deputy ministers and directors of autonomous state agencies.[3] Radical change in the top bureaucratic echelon gives the appearance of diffusion of power in Saudi Arabia and in fact some observers of the Saudi system have reached this conclusion.[4] However, public policy is the monopoly of the Saudi family. Commoners directing technical departments act as super-clerks to the royal family and serve at the latter's pleasure. Important political and security positions such as defense, interior, and foreign affairs are still held by the princes. What Ibrahim al-Awaji, a student of Saudi Arabia, who has since joined the bureaucratic elite himself, observed in the early seventies, is still true in the early eighties. He pointed out that the top government officials were chosen by the king or powerful

princes and the bases of their selection was their loyalty
and social status.[5] "Family," another Saudi social scien-
tist observes, "expresses the formal basis of government
and administration."[6] Thus, in spite of rapid educational
development and Saudi Arabia's entrance into the modern
world arena, only half of the ministers had postsecondary
education and even fewer held bachelor degrees during
Khalid's reign.[7] The dominant criteria in their selection
were ascriptive norms and not their personal achievements.

The fundamental direction of the state is toward greater
centralization. However, as much as the economics of oil
(constituting about two-thirds of the gross domestic product) necessitates central decision making, the structure of
the government militates against it. Presently, all real and
formal power rests with the king, who as the premier is in
charge of the executive. He appoints and dismisses all the
senior officials, is the supreme commander of the military,
is, in fact, the sole legislator, and he is the highest court of
appeal.[8] The vast powers of the king rest on his control of
the oil revenues. Riyadh is where decisions regarding the
provinces are made by royal decree or royal sanction.

The Saudi government is organized such that it does
not recognize a distinction between local and central government. According to a statute issued in 1963, the country was to be divided into a tri-level hierarchy of provinces,
cities, and villages all of which were subject to Riyadh.
Theoretically, the governor-general (*hakim*) of a province,
appointed by Riyadh, was to have authority over the
Riyadh-appointed governors (*muhafiz*) in his province.
The village heads (sing. *ra'is*) were also to be chosen by
and subject to the governor of the cities in whose environs
they resided. Except for making it clear that all political authority stayed in Riyadh, the statute made nothing
else clear. The number of the provinces remained unde-
fined, and consequently, each governor and village head
has continued to deal with Riyadh on an ad hoc basis.

In the absence of rules and regulations conflicts abound, but so does the ability of the central government to make discretionary decisions. In fact, while the hierarchical relations among the governors-general, governors, and village heads is not regulated, they are individually linked, both financially and administratively, to the Ministry of Interior. Their budgets are annually included in the budget for the ministry and all local projects are under the supervision of the ministry as well.[9] Personality conflicts and the governors' fear of loss of power made other regulations that would have permitted an orderly centralization inoperative.

The government has penetrated an important area, which until recently was mostly the domain of the ulema, the religious stratum. The death in 1970 of the Grand Mufti, the highest religious authority in the country, provided an opportune occasion for King Faisal to establish the Ministry of Justice, whose functions were traditionally carried out by the religious stratum. Although judges are still mostly members of the ulema, increasing numbers of them owe their appointments to the king. At the same time what may be called administrative justice is expanding its sphere of jurisdiction. Given the limitation of Islamic law, many tribunals have sprung up within the bureaucracy to handle cases ranging from forgery to bribery, to labor and commercial disputes. There are already nine such commissions, committees, and tribunals.[10] Considering that the Saudi Arabian integration into the world economy has brought about a host of new situations that cannot be settled within the old legal framework, one may expect that administrative justice will continue to mushroom. In fact, the Ottomans dealt with the same problem in the same manner in the late nineteenth century.

However, centralization of the government, in the absence of a system of specific rules and a bureaucratic class that would uphold those rules and maintain a sense of esprit de corps, is inherently destabilizing. Recruitments into the bureaucracy are carried out politically and through personal connections. No entrance examinations are envisaged for the top one-third of the bureaucracy and examinations for the lower two-thirds are provided for according to the civil service code but, in practice, they are not administered. In fact, because admission to the bureaucracy is not secured by a body of rules and regulations, but rather depends on personal connections with the minister in charge, the bureaucracy is devoid of coherence.

Many able senior officials have left public service. Discouraged by the difficulty of further promotions because of the remarkable longevity of the ministerial tenures and increasing competition for the top positions, they are easily lured away by the private sector.[11] Many young and ambitious men are drawn by the attractions of the private sector and never become public servants. Those who have chosen government service manifest serious disciplinary problems. According to a study carried out by the Saudi Institute for Public Administration, absenteeism is rampant among middle-level bureaucrats who were the subject of the study. Late arrivals and early departures are equally serious problems.[12] Many bureaucrats are employed in other remunerative capacities and conceive of their positions as secondary jobs or as payments for what the government owes them as Saudi citizens. Many other government functionaries are in fact otiose and see no reason to dedicate themselves to jobs that do not exist.

The absence of bureaucratic conditions make effective centralization improbable. One should add to this the unwillingness of the decision makers to delegate authority to their subordinates. Absence of authority to initiate programs naturally has led to inertia. Innovation and acceptance of responsibility, on the other hand, would lead to conflict with more powerful individuals. The few decision makers at the top are indeed so fearful that the apparatus of the government may be used against them that they have seen to it that the bureaucracy, as well as the military, is fragmented. This is not a unique phenomenon. Patrimonial systems often seek to subject the totality of the society to the authority of the patrimonial prince. But they are unwilling and often unable to meet the preconditions for building a centralized state. When the prince finally succeeds in becoming the center of the whole society, unprepared for the task and unsupported by a professional bureaucracy, he often succumbs under the burden he has earned.

The sums spent on the education of the Saudis and the integration of Arabia into the international system is, however, slowly producing a class of technocrats. Rather than filtering them through the older bureaucratic structure, the Saudis have utilized them to build a second bureaucracy. The Ottomans tried to do the very same thing in the nineteenth century and failed. Rather than restructuring the old institutions they attempted to build new ones paralleling the old ones. The conflict between the two was severe and the empire suffered as a consequence. Already in Saudi Arabia, the more able, ambitious, and educated bureaucrats have opted for the al-Mu'assisat al-'Am, or the public corporations, where the salary scale, prestige, and working conditions are higher and better than the old bureaucracy. Manned mostly by graduates of American universities, they handle the funding of government projects. They run the gamut of financial activities, from the Real Estate Fund to the Central Bank, from the Contractors' Fund to Social Security. There are two types of public corporations: the ones that are of security importance like the Intelligence Department or those that affect the religious sentiments of the population such as the Religious Guidance Department or the General Department of Girls

Education; and, finally, there are those that are linked to the king and perform judicial functions like the Grievance Board and Disciplinary and Investigation Board. They are directly under the authority of the monarch as they are placed either directly under the supervision of the president of the Council of Ministers, a position held by the monarch since 1964 or they are branches of the royal bureaus. There is a second type of public corporation that is linked to the regular ministries. Many of these are headed by strong executives with direct access to the king or the crown prince. In such cases the minister in charge can exercise little if any authority. The examples of this type abound and include such major autonomous institutions as the Saudi Arabian Monetary Agency (SAMA), the Institute for Public Administration, the General Organization for Petroleum and Minerals, and the University of Riyadh and the other universities. The crucial Industrial Research and Development Center is also one such agency.[13]

With the proliferation of these public bodies, the attraction of the private sector, and the limited number of educated Saudis, one cannot anticipate major improvement in the cadres of the regular bureaucracy. In the context of Saudi politics and in light of the experience of other countries, one may anticipate the deterioration of the public corporations into private bailiwicks for the purpose of personal aggrandizement.

It is safe to assume that for the next few years the public corporations will be able to absorb young educated Saudis, co-opt them through high salaries, and satisfy some of their desires for participation in nation building. The disgruntled elements, leaning toward the left, such as Dr. Ghazi al-Qusaibi, minister of industry, Hasan al-Mashari, minister of agriculture under Faisal, and Professor 'Abd al-Rahman Zamil, the deputy-minister for commerce have been co-opted in the past through attractive government positions. However, the numbers of the educated and the degree of political consciousness is increasing much too rapidly for co-optation to work for long. The present generation takes financial rewards and the availability of official positions for granted. What they look for is political efficacy. The present bureaucratic structure will not satisfy their needs and requirements. The national budget of 1981–82, allocated $7.83 billion for education.[14] Although much of this will be spent on construction, furniture, and pure waste, it is still a substantial amount in the context of the small population. It will, of necessity, foster a large educated class who will not be as easily absorbed as the few educated individuals of the past.

A more meaningful effort than the creation of the public corporations has been the movement toward administrative devolution under the direction of Dr. Ibrahim al-Awaji. Local councils appointed by the minister of interior and consisting of representatives from the central government and from each province are expected to be set up with broad powers for administering the provinces and overseeing funds.[15] Whether the decentralization program is going to work remains to be seen. The experience of other developing countries indicates that local officials are normally more corrupt and less competent than officials in the capital. To this, one must add the fear of the Saudi regime of delegating authority and their paranoia about possible threats to their rule. In spite of the prevailing odds, should the decentralization be allowed to operate, it will be an effective way to mobilize the support of the ordinary Saudi subjects. In a more developed form it may become a basis of support for the regime and may protect the regime from more radical demands for change.

The indications so far are not encouraging. Devolution in many instances has meant the further subjection of the periphery to the decisions made in Riyadh. Mu-

nicipalities (*baladiat*) are put under the authority of the
minister of municipalities and rural affairs. They can be established, adjusted, and abolished through decisions made
at the ministry. The local councils, according to the Mu-
nicipal Ordinance, are half elected and half appointed by
the minister.[16] The head of the council, equivalent to a
mayor, is an appointee of the minister and reports to the
ministry.[17] The council depends on the ministry for the
allocation of the budget and, in fact, most of the local
projects are carried out by the branches of the central
government, which have offices throughout the country.

The tribal groups, the Bedouins, are facing a similar situation. Once semiautonomous, they are now under
the authority of the Ministry of Interior, which has established the Department of Bedouin Development to handle
Bedouin administration and "all aspects of Bedouin development policy and programs."[18] The pillars of the Saudi
regime, are now dependent on the central government decisions in regard to agricultural, educational, and health
policies.

THE MILITARY STRUCTURE

The need for rapid modernization of the armed forces became apparent in 1962 when the Egyptian Air Force, giv-
ing aid to the republicans in the Yemeni civil war, strafed
the southern parts of Saudi Arabia, which had extended
assistance to the monarchists. In 1969 and 1973, the southern border posts were attacked again by the forces of the
People's Democratic Republic of Yemen (PDRY). In response to the earlier violation of Saudi sovereignty, a joint
Anglo-American commission was formed in 1965 to mod-
ernize the country's meager armed forces. Given the vul-
nerability of Saudi Arabia to Egyptian air attacks, the
Saudis were primarily interested in an air defense sys-

tem. The British agreed to sell Lightning interceptors, radar, and communication systems. The American role was limited to the sale of Hawk missile batteries, which was carried out commercially between the Saudi government and Raytheon Corporation. The U.S. role in Saudi defense build up was further reduced as a consequence of the U.S. support for Israel in the 1967 Arab-Israeli war. During the next decade, however, the situation was dramatically changed. Sophisticated military purchases replaced the earlier modest procurements and Saudi defense planning and implementation became linked with the U.S. interests in the region.

Like most of the third world countries in tension ridden regions, Saudi Arabia spends an inordinate amount of its national income on military modernization programs; but unlike most other third world countries, Saudi Arabia can afford this expenditure. In 1972, before the spiraling of oil prices, the Saudi Arabian defense budget was $839 million. Four years later, in 1976, the budget for defense stood at $8,933 million, a figure that accounted for more than a tenfold increase.[19] The lion's share of the national budget was already devoted to defense in 1974 when military expenditure accounted for 26 percent of the total budget.[20] Considering that the national economy and the national budget are almost synonymous, 26 percent represents a very large figure. Still larger increases in defense expenditures came later. It has been estimated that during the fiscal year 1980–81, $20,580 million would be allocated to military expenditure (see table 1).

A large portion of the military expenditure can be related to the U.S. foreign military sales to Saudi Arabia, which quadrupled immediately after the quadrupling of oil prices. The purchase price for U.S. military equipment, services, and construction jumped from $625.9 million in 1973 to $2,539.4 million in 1974. Traditionally, about

TABLE 1

The Saudi Arabian Defense Budget
(*In millions*)

Fiscal Year	U.S. Dollars
1973–74	988
1974–75	1,450
1975–76	6,510
1976–77[a]	10,360
1977–78[a]	11,569
1978–79[a]	13,000
1979–80[a]	14,268
1980–81[a]	20,580

SOURCE: U.S. Congress, House Committee on Foreign Affairs, Subcommittee on Europe and the Middle East, *Saudi Arabia and the United States: The New Context in an Evolving "Special Relationship,"* 97th Cong., 1st sess. (Washington, D.C.: GPO, 1981), p. 44.
[a] Estimated

80 percent of the sales consists of nonhardware material, such as training, service, and construction. For example, as much as 50 percent of the total sale has been devoted to construction of military projects.[21] According to a study by the U.S. Senate, the Saudis spent $30 billion from 1973 to 1982 for military improvements (see table 2).

The large military expenditure, the highest in the world on a per capita basis, is mostly spent on infrastructure. As of 1975, it has been reported that 85 pecent of the military budget was spent on construction. A firm in North Carolina alone had an order of one billion dollars to supply furniture for the Department of Defense.[22]

The "special relation" between the United States and Saudi Arabia is particularly pronounced in defense matters. Half of the U.S. Army Corps of Engineers' contracts are with the Saudi Arabian government, and these involve major military construction projects such as the King Khalid Military City in al-Batin near the Iraqi bor-

TABLE 2

Saudi Arabian Military
Improvement Programs, 1973–82
(*In billion $ US*)

FMS Program Approved to 1977	
Peace Hawk (F-5E)	2.8
Army mechanization	1.4
National Guard modernization	1.9
Naval expansion	3.1
Other	3.5
Subtotal	12.7[a]
Non-FMS Programs	
Army air defense	7.9
French armor	2.0
C-150 and other programs	3.5
Subtotal	13.4
Current Plans for Future Programs	
Army mechanization	1.5
Army helicopters	.1
Advanced fighters	2.5
Other	?
Subtotal	4.1
Total	30.1

SOURCE: U.S. Congress, Senate Committee on Foreign Relations, *The Sale of F-15's to Saudi Arabia*, 95th Cong., 2d sess. (Washington, D.C.: GPO, 1978), p. 243.

[a] $8.1 billion is Corps of Engineers construction.

der, which upon completion will cost $3,378 million. The Corps' projects under planning as of October 1976 came to $16,944 million. Given overruns, it is estimated that the cost will be around $20 billion.[23]

The Saudi Arabian armed forces, including the paramilitary forces, total about one hundred thousand. They are divided into five organizations with little coordination, wildly varying strengths, and unequal support from the government. The minister of defense and aviation, Prince Sultan Ibn 'Abd al-'Aziz supervises the Royal Saudi Army, the Royal Saudi Air Force, and the Royal Saudi Navy. The Saudi Arabian National Guard, often referred to as the "White Army," is under the supervision of Prince 'Abd Allah Ibn 'Abd al-'Aziz, Sultan's half brother. The frontier forces, including the Coast Guard, numbering about twelve thousand, are under the supervision of the minister of interior, Prince Na'if Ibn 'Abd al-'Aziz, Sultan's full brother.

The army is the largest of the Saudi forces, numbering some forty-five thousand men. The air force and the navy are considerably smaller, numbering fifteen thousand and three thousand each. The navy is, in fact, negligible. It does not have a flotilla or squadron organization.[24] The air force, however, has modernized and improved its performance. As of 1973, Saudi Arabia did not have advanced fighter jets. Fifty F-86s and Lightnings constituted the bulk of Saudi air power. By 1977, the Saudi air force had purchased seventy-nine F-5Es and F-5Fs, which enabled it to enter the era of advanced fighters. Still, Saudi Arabia remained a distant third in the Persian Gulf arms race, far behind Iran and Iraq.[25] In 1981, the first of the sixty F-15s, which had their offensive capabilities stripped and their flight range reduced from 2,800 to a mere 450 miles, were delivered to the government of Saudi Arabia. Moreover, the Saudis were prohibited from stationing them at the northwestern military town of Tabuq because of its proximity to Israel.[26] In 1981, many of the original restrictions on F-15s were lifted and the Saudis were permitted to purchase fighters equipped with the airborne warning and control system (AWACS).

The army is dispersed among four military cantonments where recruits are practically cut off from association with civilians. Each military cantonment contains lo-

The Saudi Arabian Military Establishment

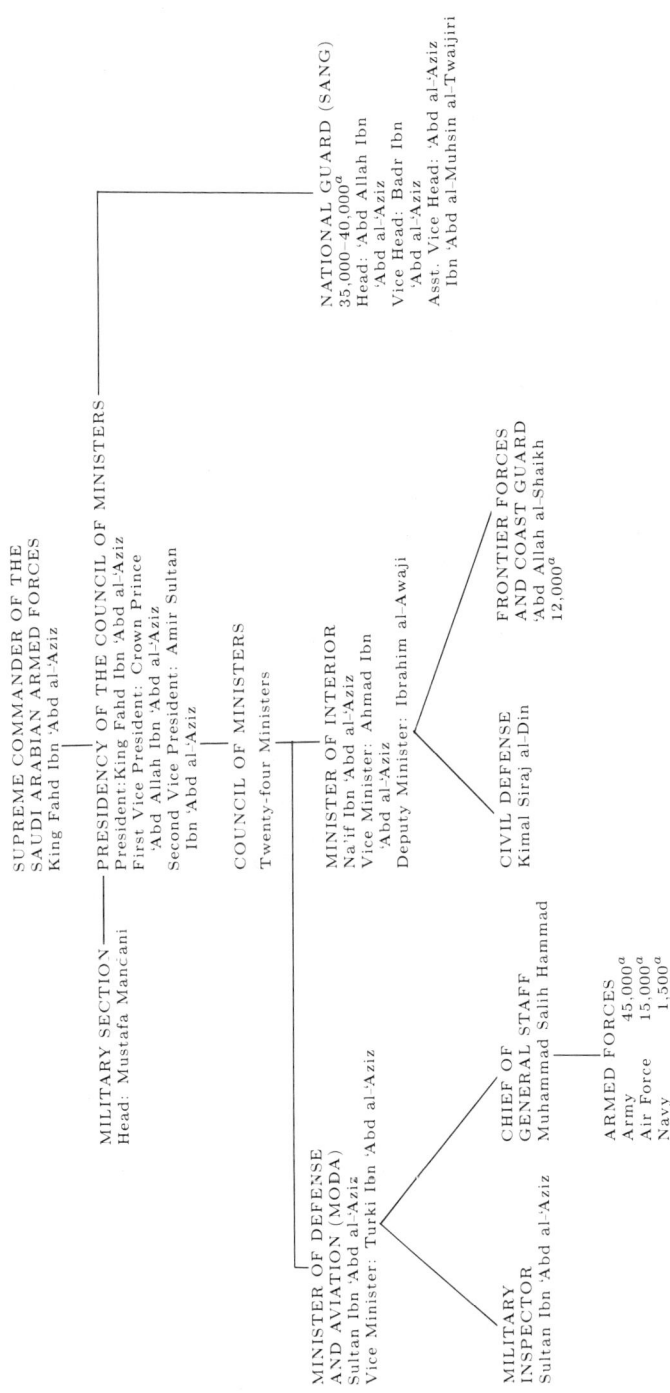

SUPREME COMMANDER OF THE
SAUDI ARABIAN ARMED FORCES
King Fahd Ibn 'Abd al-'Aziz

PRESIDENCY OF THE COUNCIL OF MINISTERS
President: King Fahd Ibn 'Abd al-'Aziz
First Vice President: Crown Prince
'Abd Allah Ibn 'Abd al-'Aziz
Second Vice President: Amir Sultan
Ibn 'Abd al-'Aziz

MILITARY SECTION
Head: Mustafa Mancani

COUNCIL OF MINISTERS
Twenty-four Ministers

MINISTER OF INTERIOR
Na'if Ibn 'Abd al-'Aziz
Vice Minister: Ahmad Ibn
'Abd al-'Aziz
Deputy Minister: Ibrahim al-Awaji

NATIONAL GUARD (SANG)
35,000–40,000[a]
Head: 'Abd Allah Ibn
'Abd al-'Aziz
Vice Head: Badr Ibn
'Abd al-'Aziz
Asst. Vice Head: 'Abd al-'Aziz
Ibn 'Abd al-Muhsin al-Twaijiri

CIVIL DEFENSE
Kimal Siraj al-Din

FRONTIER FORCES
AND COAST GUARD
'Abd Allah al-Shaikh
12,000[a]

MINISTER OF DEFENSE
AND AVIATION (MODA)
Sultan Ibn 'Abd al-'Aziz
Vice Minister: Turki Ibn 'Abd al-'Aziz

MILITARY
INSPECTOR
Sultan Ibn 'Abd al-'Aziz

CHIEF OF
GENERAL STAFF
Muhammad Salih Hammad

ARMED FORCES
Army   45,000[a]
Air Force   15,000[a]
Navy   1,500[a]

SOURCES: House Committee on Foreign Affairs, *United States Arms Policies*, pp. 245–51; House Subcommittee on Europe and the Middle East, *Saudi Arabia and the United States*, p. 46.

[a] Estimated strength

gistics and training, as well as housing and shopping facilities for the recruits and their families. These cantonments are defended by surface to air missiles and some contain airbases. The four military towns include Tabuq, Hafar al-Batin (King Khalid Military City), in the northeast, close to the Iraqi and Kuwaiti borders; Asad, in al-Kharj southeast of Riyadh; and Khamis Mushait in the southwestern province of Asir, some sixty miles north of the borders of the Yemen Arab Republic.

The army is composed of two armored brigades, one equipped with French AMX-30 tanks and one to be equipped with U.S. M-60 A1 tanks, four infantry brigades, two paratroop battalions, three artillery battalions, and a tribally recruited Royal Guard battalion. The mechanization of two infantry brigades was completed in 1980 with the help of the United States at the cost of US $1.5 billion.[27] The army is exceptionally top heavy. Its officers corps numbers twelve thousand. As a consequence of urbanization and economic prosperity, there are few Saudis who are willing to accept the military hardship and low social standing of an ordinary recruit. Thus, the military suffers from a high rate of absence without leave and manifests little discipline. The size of the military cannot be considerably enlarged. The total population of the country, about 4.5 million, is small and this includes only about one million males between the ages of eighteen and sixty.[28] Given that the literacy rate is between 5 and 20 percent, increased modernization of the military is a serious problem. Attracting the literate and the able to the military will undoubtedly create bottlenecks in the economy as the tribal sources for recruits dry up. Furthermore, increasing dependence on the urban areas for recruits may entail political risks.

Not only is the military small, particularly in view of the size of the country it has to defend, it is also technically too backward to utilize modern technology. To put down the seizure of the mosque at Mecca in 1979, the regime had to call on Jordan for assistance. The military is also intentionally immobilized. The patrimonial ruler often ensures political stability by downgrading all potential sources of threat. In view of Arab politics, a modern nationalistic armed force would certainly pose a threat to the regime. The military has been made incapable of any initiative; regiments and brigades cannot even communicate with each other. All communication must go through headquarters at Riyadh. Small, fragmented, immobilized, and technically backward, the military is not likely to stage a coup, and yet it cannot be relied upon to defend the state.

Politically the more significant force is the National Guard, which is led by Prince 'Abd Allah, a rival of Prince Sultan, who as the minister of defense directs the regular military. The National Guard traces its history to 'Abd al-'Aziz's tribal army whose loyalty and allegiance was to him and not to the state. With the destruction of the Ikhwan in 1930, some Ikhwan members shifted their allegiance from their own tribal leaders to the Saudis. This tradition of personal and traditional loyalty continues to this day. Each enlisted man is recommended in writing by the sheik of his tribe. All officers are promoted by the king himself. The National Guard is so trusted that it is placed between the regular army units and population centers. Trained by Vietnam veterans employed by the Vinnell Corporation of California, they are a well-armed, competent, and privileged group. Because they consider themselves members of the ruling class, it is unlikely they would commit any antiregime acts. But there are reports that a few of the rebels who participated in the mosque incident of 1979 were National Guard members and that their arms were stolen from the state armory.

The National Guard numbers between thirty-five and forty thousand. This figure, however, has to be taken cautiously. Many of the guards are only on part-time duty.

Theoretically the National Guard consists of forty battalions. In fact, only seventeen of them are organized and operational units. In spite of a great expenditure of money, the level of experience and education of the guards has remained low.[29] Because of U.S. modernization efforts, which began in 1973, the guards have developed four trained and equipped mechanized infantry battalions at a cost of $487.93 million, representing an 80 percent cost overrun. Vinnell Corporation carried out the training; Cadillac-Gage was responsible for vehicles; and General Electric provided the Vulcan guns.[30]

Just as the civil administration is not an integrated force, neither is the military structure. There are no contacts between the National Guard and the Ministry of Defense forces. So fearful are the Saudis of an integrated force that it was not until 1946, under the British and American influence, that they brought some of their scattered forces together and formed the Defense Ministry. Even after the Ministry of Defense was created, the politics of rule through fragmentation continued. The sheer size of the country has helped in the geographical dispersion of troops. However, the Saudis have seen to it that some of their own troops are stationed outside their borders to minimize the possibility of a coup. Increasingly, they have come to depend on foreign military forces—American military advisers or Pakistani troops—who of course pose no political threat to the regime.[31]

THE RELIGIOUS STRUCTURE

In his struggle against the Ikhwan, 'Abd al-'Aziz allied himself with religiously powerful families mostly from Hejaz. Dependent on the monarch's subsidies and fearful of the tribes, so far they have loyally supported the monarchy. The chief religious supporter of the Saudi regime has been the Shaikh family, descendants of 'Abd al-Wahhab, who have held onto the position of minister of justice and controlled the Ministry of Pilgrimage and Endowments, and the Organization for Promoting Good and Discouraging Evil (OPGDE).[32] The Ministry of Justice applies the ulema's concept of Islamic justice in a discretionary, case-by-case manner. OPGDE is, in fact, a religious police force. Other areas such as girls' education, the Religious Guidance Department, two Islamic universities, and the Great Mosque come under the authority of the ulema. Given the religious sentiments in Arabia, and the Saudis' claim to legitimacy as the protector of Islam's holiest shrines, the regime has been cautious in its dealings with the ulema. Before instituting any change, their approval is wisely sought. For example, during the 1979 incident at Mecca, before sending troops into the Great Mosque where combat is forbidden, King Khalid asked for and received an authorization from the ulema. In an earlier episode, the ulema recognized the legality of Saud's forced abdication and the succession of Faisal in 1964.[33]

There has been close unity of purpose between the Shaikh family and the Saud family. Intermarriages have brought the two families closer. King Faisal's mother, for instance, was a member of the Shaikh family. The ulema are respected by the royal family and their requests and wishes are often complied with. No fundamental changes are likely to take place without the ulema's approval. In contrast to the tribal chiefs who are fragmented into local interests, the ulema form a cohesive group.

The ulema consider themselves the guardians of the Islamic value system. Shaikh 'Abd Allah, the head of the ulema, has expressed concern that "blind and ignorant imitation of Western ways and ideas" may harm Saudi society.[34] King Fahd, like his predecessor King Khalid, regularly meets with the ulema. Rumors about Fahd's

character, however, may cast him in a hypocritical light
and deprive him of traditional legitimacy. In the long run,
however, given the tempo of change and the increasingly
important role that the state has come to play in pene-
trating the society on one hand, and the conservativism of
the ulema on the other, conflict will be inevitable.

The influence of the ulema, while quite substantial,
is often exaggerated. They have remained, to a large extent, apolitical. On the two occasions when they made major political decisions, namely Saud's abdication and the
seizure of the Great Mosque at Mecca, they did so upon
the request of the actual holders of power. They simply legitimized actions that the government would have taken in
any case. When they opposed the spread of certain cultural
and social innovations, such as the use of the Georgian calendar to draw up economic plans, the change to Greenwich
mean time, the spread of secular education for girls, and
the introduction of television, they failed to persuade the
government to alter its course.[35] While the conversions to
the Georgian calendar and Greenwich mean time seem in-
nocuous, one must bear in mind that they affect a series of
religious practices arranged around lunar movement and
the clock. The Georgian calendar negates the importance
of the first Islamic government in Medina, which is the
basis of all Islamic calendars. In these areas, as well as
in the field of adjudication, the state has undermined the
power of the ulema.

In fact, from the beginning, the Saudi family antici-
pated the possibility of conflict with the ulema, its traditional allies. Therefore, the Saudis saw to it that the ulema
were not in an effective position to oppose the royal family.
Consequently, the OPGDE was divided into two distinct
groups, each headed by a rival branch of the Shaikh family.
These public morality committees are in charge of administering religious laws. Because Islam is conceived as a total

system, their authority to interfere in an individual's life is almost unlimited. The OPGDE has given the Saudis an institutional means to penetrate the society and identify disloyalty while buttressing their own legitimacy as devout Muslims. However, the excesses of the OPGDE eventually may cause conflict between the regime and its growing Westernized population. What is interesting is that the regime has ensured that the religious police, just like the civil and military bureaucracy, is fragmented and unable to oppose the regime as a united front.[36]

One may conclude that the regime is inherently unable to mobilize any kind of active and powerful support. It aims toward pacification and fragmentation of the society rather than generating support. Any state that has to weaken its own bases in order to minimize political threat is in a very weak and unstable position.

In the past fifty years, the Saudis have not developed any viable institutional support for their regime. The early institutions, which 'Abd al-'Aziz helped to create, have been either weakened or are outmoded. In fact, from the very beginning the system was based on personal alliances and not institutional arrangements. The integration of Arabia into the world market has had a revolutionary effect on the structure of Arabian society. Modern social forces have come into existence.[37] The fragmented society, under the impact of oil, is becoming increasingly united. At the same time, the level of conflict is bound to grow. Expanding contact between individuals and groups, conflict over the distribution of economic goods, contests over various concepts of state organization will all put a burden on the state. No organization exists at the moment to channel such political demands in an orderly institutionalized manner.

3

Economic Growth
and Structural Change

During the past two decades, the growth of Saudi Arabia's revenues from the export of petroleum has been remarkable. The oil revenues received by the Saudi government increased from $334 million in 1960 to $84.5 billion in 1980. This two-hundred-and-fiftyfold increase was caused by the rapid growth of output and the dramatic increase in the price of oil. Between 1960 and 1980, the kingdom's annual oil output increased from 481 million barrels to 3,624 million barrels, and the price of its light crude increased from $1.80 to $32.00 per barrel.[1] As a consequence of the growth of its oil income, Saudi Arabia was transformed in two decades from one of the poorest countries of the world into a highly prosperous nation. In 1980, the kingdom's per capita gross national product (GNP) of $11,260 was the twelfth highest in the world, ranking above such countries as England, Austria, and Japan.[2]

The direct effects of oil exports on income in Saudi Arabia are shown in table 3. Between 1970 and 1980, about three-quarters of the increase in domestic income was caused by the improvement in the kingdom's terms of trade. The growth of petroleum output contributed another 11 percent to the expansion of income. On the other hand, despite the non-oil economy's high rate of growth, it accounted for less than one-sixth of the rise in income during the period under consideration.

TABLE 3

Sources of Growth of Domestic Income, 1970–80
(*At constant 1970 prices*)

Sources of Growth	Million Riyals	Percentages of Total
Expansion of non-oil economy	17,709	14.4
Expansion of petroleum sector	14,100	11.4
Terms of trade effect	91,343	74.2
Total increase in domestic income	123,152	100.0

SOURCE: Table A-8, Appendix A.

The indirect economic effects of oil exports have also been noteworthy. Oil revenues have provided the resources for large-scale investment and educational expenditures, and a massive importation of labor from abroad. Investment expenditures and the expansion of the educational system have contributed to the rise of labor productivity, and the inflow of foreign workers has significantly augmented the supply of labor in the kingdom. The growth of manpower and the rise of productivity have combined to generate a rapid expansion of the non-oil economy. Between 1967 and 1980, the labor force engaged in activities other than petroleum production and refining increased from 1,290,000 to 2,520,000; and annual output per worker increased from 4,180 to 8,850 Saudi riyals (SR), at constant 1970 prices. The non-oil gross domestic product (GDP) expanded at an average annual rate of 11.5 percent during the same period.[3] A major cause of the growth of the labor force has been the influx of expatriate workers (see table 4). By 1980, according to official estimates, 43 percent of the supply of civilian manpower was made up of non-Saudis. Since a very small percentage of foreign workers are engaged in agriculture, their share in nonagricultural employment is probably higher than 55 percent.[4]

TABLE 4

Employment by Nationality, 1967 and 1980
(*Civilian employment only*)

Nationality	Thousands		Percentages of Total	
	1967	1980	1967	1980
Saudi	1027	1411	81	57
Non-Saudi	240	1060	19	43
Total	1267	2471	100	100

SOURCES: Table A-6, Appendix A; K.O.S.A., Ministry of Planning, *The Third Development Plan 1400–1405 (1980–1985)* (Riyadh: Ministry of Planning, 1980), p. 98; J. S. Birks and C. A. Sinclair, *Arab Manpower, The Crisis of Development* (London: Croom Helm, 1980), p. 107.

TABLE 5

Sources of Growth of Non-oil GDP, 1967–80
(*At constant 1970 factor prices*)

Sources of Growth	Million Riyals	Percentages of Total
Rise of productivity	6,033	36
Growth of national labor force	3,681	22
Growth of nonnational labor force	7,158	42
Total increase in non-oil GDP	16,872	100

SOURCE: Table A-9, Appendix A.

The effects of the rise in labor productivity and the increased national an nonnational labor force on economic growth are summarized in table 5.[5] Between 1967 and 1980, about 36 percent of the increase in non-oil GDP was caused by the rise in labor productivity and the other 64 percent was a result of the growth of employment. The influx of workers from abroad was the source of about 42 percent of the rise in non-oil GDP. It should be noted that the data in table 5 underestimate the contribution of expatriate workers for two reasons. First, because of insufficient data, it was assumed that military manpower is made up totally of Saudi nationals. Second, the effect of foreign manpower on productivity was not included in the computations. Since the nonnationals are generally more skilled than the nationals, the increase in the share of the former in the labor force automatically raises the average level of labor productivity.

Not only have oil revenues stimulated a rapid growth of production outside the petroleum industry, they have also had a major impact on the structure of non-oil economic activity. Since the growing oil revenues have greatly expanded the capacity to import tradable goods (agricultural and industrial products), domestic economic activity has shifted toward the production of those goods and services that cannot be imported from abroad (nontradables). The non-oil GDP was dominated by nontradables as early as 1967. This dominance has increased as the share of agriculture has continued to decline and the share of industry has failed to increase substantially. As a consequence, in 1980, nontradables accounted for about 85 percent of the non-oil GDP. The increase in the share of nontradables has been caused mainly by the rapid growth of construction, commerce, and transportation (table 6).

The mirror image of the inadequate development of the tradable sectors is excessive dependence on imports. In fact, other than a few oil-exporting city-states, such as Kuwait and the United Arab Emirates, it is difficult to find a country that is as dependent on imports as Saudi Arabia. Although as early as 1965 the share of imports

in total domestic supply was quite high, it experienced
a notable increase in the 1970s. By 1977, total domestic
supply was SR 72 billion and SR 51 billion of these goods
and services were imported from abroad.[6] In 1980, the

TABLE 6

Structure of Non-oil GDP, 1967 and 1980
(*At constant 1970 factor prices*)

Sector	Million Saudi Riyals 1967	1980	Percentages of Total 1967	1980
Agriculture	885	1,639	14.0	6.5
Industry[a]	467	2,473	7.4	9.8
Construction	952	5,091	15.1	20.1
Commerce[b]	1,927	9,186	30.5	36.2
Transportation[c]	435	3,031	6.9	12.0
Other private services[d]	171	611	2.7	2.4
Public services[e]	1,475	3,333	23.4	13.1
Tradables[f]	1,352	4,112	21.4	16.2
Nontradables[g]	4,960	21,252	78.6	83.8
Total	6,312	25,364	100.0	100.0

SOURCE: Table A-4, Appendix A.
NOTE: Based on the revised system of prices.

[a] Includes mining, manufacturing, and utilities.
[b] Includes trade, ownership of dwellings, finance, insurance, real estate, and business services.
[c] Also includes storage and communications.
[d] Community, social, and personal services.
[e] Includes public administration, education, health, and defense.
[f] Includes agriculture and industry.
[g] Includes all sectors other than agriculture and industry.

value of agricultural imports was three times greater than
local agricultural production and the value of industrial
imports was more than ten times greater than domestic
industrial output.[7]

Along with production, the labor force has also shifted toward sectors producing nontradables. In 1967, the combined share of construction and services in total labor force was about 40 percent. One decade later, they accounted for more than two-thirds of all employment. The sharp decline in the share of agriculture has been accompanied by a significant increase in the shares of construction, commerce, transportation, and other private services (table 7).

TABLE 7

Structure of Labor Force, 1967 and 1980
(*Excluding petroleum production and refining*)

Sector	Number of Persons (*In thousands*) 1967	1980	Percentages of Total 1967	1980
Agriculture	714	599	55.3	23.8
Industry[a]	58	143	4.5	5.7
Construction	62	330	4.8	13.1
Commerce[b]	81	345	6.3	13.7
Transportation[c]	53	215	4.1	8.5
Other private services[d]	145	482	11.2	19.1
Public services[e]	179	404	13.8	16.0
Total	1,292	2,518	100.0	99.9

SOURCES: Tables A-6, A-7, Appendix A.

[a] Includes mining, manufacturing, and utilities.
[b] Includes trade, finance, insurance, real estate, and business services.
[c] Also includes storage and communications.
[d] Community, social, and personal services.
[e] Includes both civilian and military manpower.

Another important characteristic of the labor market in Saudi Arabia is service orientation of the national manpower. Although construction employs a large percentage of the labor force outside agriculture, it is almost totally dependent on non-Saudi labor. Similarly, the number of Saudis working in the oil sector, other mining, manufacturing, and utilities is not very large. In 1975, nonservice activities employed only 16 percent of the Saudis working outside agriculture.[8] It should also be noted that a sizable proportion of the Saudi work force in urban areas is crowded in unproductive activities as independent workers. The very low level of output per worker in "other private services"–the largest employer of urban manpower–is indicative of this crowding phenomenon (table 8). In 1980,

TABLE 8

Value Added Per Worker
in Urban Activities, 1980
(Excluding petroleum production and refining)

Sector	Thousand Saudi Riyals
Industry[a]	57
Construction	130
Commerce[b]	64
Transportation	70
Other private services[c]	11
Public services	58
Total	61

SOURCES: Tables A-3, A-6, A-7, Appendix A.

[a] Includes mining, manufacturing, and utilities.
[b] Includes trade, finance, insurance, real estate, and business services. Does not include ownership of dwellings.
[c] Community, social, and personal services.

the value added per worker in other private services was SR 11,000.[9] In the same year, the average annual wage rate for Saudi production workers was about SR 30,000.[10] This indicates that many independent workers could increase their employment income significantly by offering their labor as wage earners in the organized segment of the private economy. However, in 1980, the Saudis accounted for only one-quarter of the wage labor employed in urban private establishments.[11] Some observers have attributed this contradiction to the Saudis' contempt for manual work. A more plausible explanation is probably the availability of nonemployment income to Saudi citizens in the form of direct and indirect government subsidies. It is access to "unearned incomes" that has made low-level, blue-collar employment unattractive for the unskilled and semiskilled Saudis and has allowed them to withdraw their labor from those activities where they could be socially productive.

4

Social Transformation

The change in the structure of the economy is only one aspect of the impact of oil wealth upon Saudi Arabia. The rapid growth of oil income has also had a profound effect upon the society. An examination of the social transformation of the kingdom during the past twenty years is essential for a thorough understanding of its present and future. The most important aspects of this transformation have been rapid urbanization, diffusion of education among the population, altered class structure, increased contact with the outside world, heightened political awareness due to the growth of communications, and elevated materialistic expectations. This section is devoted to the study of these important phenomena.

URBANIZATION

Because of the shortage of water and the use of primitive agricultural techniques, Saudi agriculture is very unproductive and, consequently, rural income is very low. On the other hand, oil income has created enormous opportunities for workers in urban areas. In 1980, average annual output per worker (gross value added per worker) in agriculture was 7.8 thousand riyals while output per worker in nonagricultural activities other than oil was 60.8 thousand riyals,[1] or eight times greater. The large gap between urban and rural incomes has, therefore, created a massive flow of rural population into the cities. Another cause of the high rate of urban drift has been the increased supply of social services provided by the government in urban areas. The educational opportunities available in the cities have been a major force attracting the young rural Saudis to large metropolitan centers. In 1960, the urban share of the total population in Saudi Arabia was 30 percent, while in Iran it was 34 percent. Twenty years later, urban expansion in the kingdom had surpassed that in Iran. In 1980, two-thirds of the Saudi population lived in cities; while in Iran, the urban centers accounted for 50 percent of the total population.[2] In addition to a rapid rate of migration from the countryside to the cities, the urban population has also become more concentrated. In 1962–63 the three cities of Riyadh, Jidda, and Mecca accounted for 28 percent of the urban population; their share in 1974 had reached 40 percent.[3] While the share of the three largest cities in urban population is about equal in Saudi Arabia and Iran, there exists a major difference between the large urban areas in the two countries.[4] Unlike Iran, the distribution of population among the three major Saudi Arabian cities is fairly equal. In 1976 the population of Tehran was about seven times greater than that of Iran's second largest city (Isfahan).[5] In contrast, in 1974, the population of Riyadh was not even twice that of Saudi Arabia's *third* largest city (Mecca).[6] Therefore, it is unlikely that any of the major Saudi cities play as dominant a role in the national politics as Tehran has played in the political life of Iran.

EDUCATION

Since the beginning of the First Development Plan (1970–75), economic growth has been a major goal of the Saudi state. The pursuit of this goal has generated a sizable demand for professional, managerial, and technical manpower. This demand has been satisfied mainly through importation of workers from abroad. However, to reduce dependence on foreign labor, the state has given a high priority to manpower development.

The record since the early 1970s has been rather impressive. The number of schools at different levels of education increased 150 percent during the short period between 1972 and 1980; and school enrollment more than doubled during the same period. The growth of enrollment at the secondary level has been especially noteworthy. The number of secondary students nearly quadrupled between 1972 and 1980 (table 9).

TABLE 9

Number of Schools and Students,
1971–72 and 1979–80

	Schools		Students (*In thousands*)	
	1971–72	1979–80	1971–72	1979–80
Primary	2,154	5,373	475	862
Intermediate	484	1,377	84	245
Secondary	148	456	24	94
Teacher Training Institutes	65	107	15	22
Special education	10	25	1	2
Total	2,861	7,338	599	1,225

SOURCES: U.N., *The Population Situation,* pp. 11.15, 11.16; K.O.S.A., *The Statistical Indicators 1980,* pp. 169–74.

Because of its late start in educational development, Saudi Arabia still has to rely on foreign teachers in its educational system. Dependence on foreign teachers is especially significant at the higher levels of education. In 1980, 77 percent of the teachers in intermediate schools and 83 percent of those in secondary schools were non-Saudis. At the elementary level, non-Saudis accounted for 35 percent of the total teaching staff.[7] The expatriate teachers are likely to play a very important role as agents of social change. Of course it many be argued that since they are primarily from other Arab countries, their values are not significantly different from those existing in the kingdom. However, it should be noted that, with few exceptions, the process of social change started much earlier in other Arab countries, and their intelligentsia is likely to be far more secular and modern than those in Saudi Arabia.[8] Some observers have noted that, in fact, of the high-level foreign manpower in Saudi Arabia, those from other Arab countries are far less tolerant of the traditional Saudi culture than are Westerners.

Advisors and other agents of change from similar cultures within the Muslim world are often less respectful of the indigenous context in which they work than are foreigners from a totally different society. An Egyptian fresh from the cafe society of Cairo or a Lebanese from Beruit's al-Hamrah may look with disdain on Saudi austerity and be impatient with the consequent life-style. On the other hand, non-Moslem westerners, such as Americans or Britons, may find nostalgic relief and antiquarian charm in the very Saudi milieu. Reactions of some Egyptian, Jordanian, Pakistani and Palestinian workers in Saudi Arabia tend to validate this observation.[9]

The growth of higher education has also been noteworthy. In the early 1950s, Saudi Arabia did not have a university. The opening of Riyadh University in 1957 was followed by the founding of three others in the 1960s; three more were established in the 1970s.[10] Between 1972 and 1980, the number of departments at Saudi universities increased from nineteen to fifty-one. Enrollment at these universities increased from 9,500 to 48,000 during the same period.[11] In addition to the growing opportunities for university education at home, thanks to the oil income, a growing number of young Saudis have been able to go abroad for higher education. In 1980, 10,035 Saudis were studying abroad. More than three-quarters of these students were attending universities in the United States and Europe. The U.S. universities alone were educating 6,896 Saudi students.[12] Those students who are studying at Saudi universities are mainly in social sciences, humanities, law, education, and commerce. Those who are studying abroad major predominately in sciences and engineering.[13]

As a result of the growth of higher education, a new professional middle class is emerging in Saudi Arabia, which is likely to become quite powerful both in its numerical strength, and its control over the economy. This class is likely to demand participation in economic and political decision making. However, as will be shown later, this class is still very small and is not likely to become an important social force until the 1990s.

Despite the recent advances in the educational system, as a result of the kingdom's late move toward manpower development, the Saudi population is still mainly uneducated. Table 10 compares the enrollment ratios and the literacy rate in the kingdom to the averages for fifty-six developing countries whose per capita GNP in 1980 was higher than $410. It is apparent that, notwithstanding the very high per capita GNP in Saudi Arabia, its educational achievements do not compare favorably with those of the middle-income developing economies. In 1974, of the literate Saudi population aged ten years and over, only 17 percent had achieved more than primary education (table 11). However, given its immense wealth and the urgency of political and economic pressures, the government

TABLE 10

Education Indicators

	Saudi Arabia		Middle-income Countries[a]
	1960	1977	1977
Enrollment ratio (percentage) Primary School[b]			
Male	22	78	100
Female	2	49	92
Total	12	64	96
Secondary school[c]	2	31	44
Higher education[d]	*[e]	7	13
Literacy rate (percentage)[f]	3	16	73

SOURCE: World Bank, *World Development Report 1982,* pp. 153–54.

[a] Average for 56 developing countries with per capita GNP in 1980 higher than $410.

[b] Numbers enrolled in primary school as percentage of age group.

[c] Numbers enrolled in secondary shool as percentage of age group.

[d] Numbers enrolled in higher education as percentage of population aged 20–24.

[e] Less than 0.5 percent.

[f] Percentage of persons aged 15 and over who can read and write.

is likely to continue its present policy of educational expansion, and the Saudi society will, therefore, experience a rapid increase in literacy rate in the 1980s.

CLASS STRUCTURE

Because of the inadequate data, it is difficult to provide a detailed analysis of class structure in Saudi Arabia. However, it is possible to ascertain the size of some broadly defined social classes. To be more specific, the labor force

can be divided into three major categories: peasants and
nomads, the working class, and the middle class. The first

TABLE 11

Population Aged Ten Years and Over
by Education and Sex, 1974

Level of Education	Male	Female	Total	Male	Female	Total
	(*In thousands*)			(*In percentages*)		
Illiterate	1,047	1,496	2,543	52.5	81.2	66.3
Literate and primary	761	293	1,054	38.2	15.9	27.5
Secondary and higher	181	42	223	9.1	2.3	5.8
Not stated	4	11	15	0.2	0.6	0.4
Total	1,993	1,842	3,835	100.0	100.0	100.0

SOURCE: U.N., *The Population Situation*, p. 11.14.

group is essentially outside the market system. It is engaged in subsistence agriculture, animal husbandry and
fishing. Although members of this group are entering the
money economy as consumers through the subsidies that
they receive from the government, their productivity is so
low that they are unable to produce marketable surplus
beyond their own subsistence needs. The working class
is made up of all people who earn a major part of their
income through the exertion of their pure labor.

Included in this group are wage earners, self-employed
workers, and unpaid family workers engaged in production,
sales, transportation, and services. Finally, the middle
class is made up of those people whose major source of income is their endowment of material, or human capital (education and skills). Included in this group are managers,
officials, professionals, technicians, and clerical workers.
Unfortunately the available data do not allow the separa-
tion of this group into those whose main source of income is
human capital (professional middle class) from those who
receive their income mainly from the ownership of material

capital (bourgeoisie). But since the numerical size of the latter group is usually very small, our category of middle class is representative of that portion of the labor force whose income is mainly generated by its endowments of human capital.

As late as 1964, peasants and nomads comprised about three-quarters of the one million economically active persons in Saudi Arabia. The rest of the labor force was primarily engaged as wage earners in agriculture, small craft, construction, trade, other private services, and public services.[14] The share of the middle class in the labor force was probably not higher than 5 percent. The professional middle class was mainly employed in "cadre grades" in the public sector,[15] and in "staff" positions in the Arabian American Oil Company (Aramco). In 1962, there were about thirty-six thousand civilian public-sector employees in cadre grades,[16] but fewer than six thousand Saudis held staff positions in Aramco.[17]

Class structure in present-day Saudi Arabia is much different from that in the early 1960s (table 12). The decline in the relative numerical size of peasants and nomads and the rise of the other two classes have been substantial. However, it should be noted that table 12 includes foreign workers as well as Saudi nationals. The change in the class structure of the Saudi labor force has been less dramatic but nevertheless noteworthy (table 13). The most significant development of the past two decades has been the marked growth of the working class. By 1980, this class had become nearly as large as peasants and nomads.

Although the working class is numerically dominant in urban areas and the middle class is still rather small, this situation is not likely to continue for long. The middle class is going to grow very rapidly as a result of favorable supply and demand conditions. Because of the rise of income, availability of government subsidies, and growing educational opportunities, the supply of the educated labor force will expand significantly. In addition, because of high wages, production will be capital intensive and, therefore, demand for managerial and professional manpower will rise faster than demand for unskilled labor.

TABLE 12

Class Structure, 1980
(*Total labor force excluding military*)

Class Category	Thousands of Persons	Percentages of Total
Middle class[a]	472	19.1
Working class[b]	1,377	55.7
Peasants and nomads[c]	622	25.2
Total	2,471	100.0

SOURCE: K.O.S.A., *Third Development Plan,* p. 102.

[a] Includes managers, officials, professionals, technicians, and clerical workers.

[b] Includes production, sales, transportation, and service workers.

[c] Includes farmers, nomads, and fishermen.

TABLE 13

Class Structure, 1980
(*Employed Saudis excluding military*)

Class Category	Thousands of Persons	Percentages of Total
Middle class	195	13.8
Working class	594	42.1
Peasants and nomads	622	44.1
Total	1,411	100.0

SOURCES: K.O.S.A., *Second Development Plan,* p. 247; and *Third Development Plan,* p. 102.

As Saudi nationals gain the necessary skills and education, they will replace skilled foreign workers. This process will increase the relative size of the Saudi middle class at the expense of the working class and the peasant and nomad population. In fact, in about twenty years a very large percentage of Saudis will be in the middle and upper classes of the society while the working class will be composed mainly of foreign laborers. However, it should be emphasized that because of the very large initial size of the working class, it will continue to be the dominant class in the 1980s. The shift of power to the middle class will be a phenomenon of the 1990s.

While we do not have direct information about the size and composition of the property-owning class in the kingdom, it is possible to use the data on the distribution of private firms to gain some insight into the characteristics of this group. The Saudi business community is made up of a large number of very small firms. In 1976, medium-sized and large firms accounted for less than 5 percent of nonagricultural business (table 14). If we classify

TABLE 14

Characteristics of Private Firms in
Nonagricultural Activities, 1976

Workers Per Establishment	Number of Establishments	Percentages of Total
1	44,076	57.0
2–9	29,605	38.3
10–49	2,851	3.7
50 and over	720	0.9
Not specified	52	0.1
Total	77,304	100.0

SOURCE: K.O.S.A., *Statistical Indicators 1980*, p. 39.

those businessmen who employ fewer than nine workers as the "petty bourgeoisie" and those who employ more than nine workers as the "bourgeoisie," data in table 14 indicate that the Saudi bourgeoisie is still very small. This is not a surprising result given the underdevelopment of the productive sectors and the dominant role of the state in the kingdom's economy. Without an effort directed at transferring financial resources from the government to the private sector, the Saudi bourgeoisie is unlikely to develop as a viable social force. Consequently, the nonpropertied (professional) middle class will have the chance to become the uncontested dominant class of the future.

SOCIAL INTERACTIONS

In addition to rapid urbanization, the diffusion of education among the population, and changing class structure, there are a number of other factors that may have significant impact on the attitudes of Saudi nationals.

The first factor is the extensive contact with people from other cultures. In 1980, 43 percent of the total civilian labor force in Saudi Arabia was from other countries (see table 4). In nonagricultural occupations, expatriates comprised 73 percent of the employees in private sector establishments.[18] Although the government has continuously tried to keep the foreign workers segregated, it would be an impossible task to keep more than one million workers and their families completely separate from the indigenous population. About 50 percent of the expatriate workers are from North Yemen, but large numbers from countries as diverse as Egypt, Korea, and the United States also work in the kingdom.[19] The role of foreign teachers as agents of social change has already been discussed. While the impact of the other expatriates may not be as far-reaching as that of the teachers, their life-styles, ideas, and attitudes are likely to have an impact on their Saudi peers, especially among the more educated groups.

Contact with other cultures has also increased through foreign travel. Thanks to large oil revenues, more and more

Saudis are able to go abroad for education, vacation, and shopping. In 1972, Saudi nationals spent $160 million on foreign travel. Nine years later, in 1981, expenditure by Saudis traveling abroad had increased to $2,760 million.[20]

Communication facilities have allowed the Saudis to be more aware of events at home and abroad. Before 1960, there was a total of four newspapers and periodicals in the kingdom. By 1973, their number had jumped to twenty-nine.[21] The increase in the circulation of daily general-interest newspapers has also been remarkable. In 1976, circulation per thousand inhabitants in Saudi Arabia was 19.3, in Iran it was 14.1.[22] In 1970, in the village of Bushur, where per capita income was SR 427[23] (per capita income for the kingdom as a whole was SR 2,244 in the same year[24]), there were 214 transistor radios per thousand inhabitants.[25] In contrast, radio receivers per thousand inhabitants in Iran was only 63 in 1976.[26]

The increase in mobility within Saudi Arabia has also had a significant impact on the spread of news by "word of mouth" from one locality to another. Between 1973 and 1978, the number of registered vehicles in the kingdom increased from one per 5.4 workers to one per 1.4 workers.[27] Transmission of news and information by word of mouth is especially important in countries where the mass media is implicitly or explicitly censored by the government. For example, during the Iranian Revolution of 1978–79, taxi cabs were a major source of dissemination of news by opposition groups.

As a result of the rapid growth of national income and the increase in the level and variety of consumption, Saudi Arabia is being transformed into a consumption-oriented and materialistic society. Using per capita imports as an index of the potential strength of the demonstration effect,[28] among the major oil-exporting countries of the Middle East and North Africa,[29] Kuwait, Saudi Ara-

bia, and Libya have the greatest potential for transformation into materialistic societies (table 15).

TABLE 15

Per Capita Annual Imports of
Major Oil Exporting Countries, 1980

Country	U.S. Dollars
Kuwait	8,120
Saudi Arabia	3,360
Libya	3,330
Iraq	800
Algeria	510
Iran	320

SOURCE: World Bank, *World Development Report 1982,* pp. 111, 125.

It is obvious that greater materialism implies greater
sensitivity to inequities in distribution of income and wealth.
The Saudi leadership seems to be quite aware of the political dangers of a "consumer society" as can be seen from
the following statement by Ghazi al-Qusaibi, minister of
industry and electricity:

Great wealth carries with it the desire for a life of enjoyment and
leisure. We have already observed the emergence of a consumer society whose material requirements are endless. Spiritual restraint is
always needed but it becomes imperative in cases of rapid growth
when the individual becomes fascinated by the material attractions
of modern civilization, by the amounts of money displayed and by
the opportunities for gain whether legal or illegal within his reach.
All this we have to resist and oppose. We should go back to the purity
of our faith and abide by its principles.[30]

5

Economic Sources of
Potential Political Discontent

While the massive oil income has transformed Saudi Arabia into one of the most prosperous nations of the world, it has also generated considerable political tension within the kingdom. How the oil resources are used, and who receives the greatest benefit from them are important questions that will eventually determine the degree of conflict or harmony in Saudi society. For this reason, it is important to examine the objective factors that have the greatest potential for causing discontent among the various segments of the Saudi population. Such factors include the degree of government control over the economy, the success or failure of the state in transforming the oil wealth into productive assets, and the distribution of income among the population.

THE ROLE OF THE STATE IN THE ECONOMY

Since the income generated from the production of oil mainly accrues to the government, the public sector dominates the Saudi economy despite its free enterprise ideology. In recent years, this domination has increased dramatically, as a result of the rapid growth of oil revenues. While in 1965 government revenue was about 30 percent of GDP, by 1980 this ratio had increased to 55 percent.[1] The extensive economic power of the state is apparent from the structure of expenditures in the kingdom. Between 1975 and 1980, consumption expenditures of the government were larger than those of the private sector (table 16). In

TABLE 16

Expenditure on the GDP, 1975–80
(*At current market prices*)

Expenditure Category	SR Billions	Percentages of Total
Private consumption	262	19
Government consumption	293	21
Gross fixed capital formation	341	25
Government	(203)	(15)
Non-oil private sector	(95)	(7)
Oil sector	(43)	(3)
Increase in stocks	15	1
Net exports of goods and services	460	34
Total expenditure on GDP	1,371	100

SOURCE: Table A-5, Appendix A.

contrast, public consumption expenditures in the United States are only 28 percent of private consumption spending. In developing countries this ratio is even smaller. In Turkey and the Republic of Korea it is only 19 and 20 percent respectively.[2] In addition to the large consumption expenditures, investment spending by the Saudi government is also immense. Between 1975 and 1980, the public sector's investment in the domestic economy was more than twice that of the private sector; and a very large segment of the GDP was invested by the government outside the kingdom (table 16).

While oil income allows large expenditures for social welfare and economic development, it also makes the government ubiquitous in the national economy. As long as the share of oil revenues in national income was low, distortions, inefficiencies, and welfare losses due to governmental spending of these revenues were not significant. But now the state's income from petroleum exports is so large that one corrupt minister or one miscalculation by a government technocrat can cause major economic distortions and a large welfare loss. Naturally, in today's Saudi Arabia, the public is likely to be far less tolerant of mistakes and irregularities.

An examination of government expenditures during the Second Development Plan (1975–80), provides considerable insight into its priorities and the potential for political discontent as a consequence of its policies. The plan allocated 64 percent of government expenditures to developmental projects in areas such as infrastructure, economic resources, human resources, and social resources. Thirty-six percent of government expenditures were designated for such areas as defense, administration, and aid and subsidies (table 17). By the end of the plan, total actual disbursements were about 40 percent greater than total planned expenditures. Most of this increase was allocated to defense and some to infrastructure. While actual expenditures for defense were almost three times more than the planned level, those for economic resources were about one-half of the planned expenditures. In fact, during the Second Development Plan, the disbursements for defense and security were larger than the combined spending for economic, human, and social resources (table 17).

At present, per capita defense expenditure in Saudi Arabia is about $2,500 per year, which is about four times the level in the United States (table 18). In fact, among fifty-six countries for which 1980 defense spending data are available, the kingdom had the highest per capita defense expenditure. The country with the second highest level

TABLE 17

Fiscal Allocations in the Second Development Plan

Category	Planned Allocations SR Billions	Percentages of Total	Actual Allocations SR Billions	Percentages of Total
Development sector	<u>318</u>	<u>64</u>	<u>348</u>	<u>50</u>
Infrastructure	113	23	190	28
Economic resources	92	18	43	6
Human resources	80	26	76	11
Social resources	33	7	37	5
Nondevelopmental sector	<u>180</u>	<u>36</u>	<u>346</u>	<u>50</u>
Defense and security	78	16	212	31
Administration	38	7	35	5
External assistance food subsidies, etc.	64	13	99	14
Total	498	100	694	100

SOURCE: Chamieh, *Saudi Arabia Yearbook*, pp. 139–40.

TABLE 18

Defense Expenditures, 1980

Country	$ Million	$ Per Capita	% of GNP
Saudi Arabia	20,704	2,518	18
Israel	5,200	1,333	23
United States	142,700	644	6

SOURCES: International Institute for Strategic Studies, *The Military Balance, 1981–1982,* pp. 112–13; Saudi Arabian Monetary Agency (SAMA), *Annual Report 1981,* p. 170.

was Israel, which spent about half as much per capita.[3] Another indicator of the relative size of defense spending is the share of GNP allocated to military expenditure. This ratio in Saudi Arabia is about three times that in the United States (table 18). Compared to the income of an urban production worker of about SR 30,000 per year in 1980,[4] annual defense spending of more than SR 45,000 per employed Saudi national is clearly enormous.[5] The preference of the Saudi worker for security would have to be extremely high to find such a large defense expenditure acceptable. Because of the small size of the armed forces, very few Saudis derive direct benefit from military spending. Between 1975 and 1977, wages and salaries accounted for only 13 percent of current defense expenditures. The massive allotment of national resources to defense and security can create considerable discontent, especially among the low-income population. This public disapproval can become especially intense if the main purpose of military spending is perceived to be not the national security but the security of the ruling elite.

Another explosive issue is the degree of waste, corruption, and inefficiency in the use of oil revenues. The incremental capital-output ratio (ICOR) in the Saudi economy increased enormously after the oil price increase of 1973.[6] Comparing the periods of 1965–73 and 1973–77, a given increase in GDP required three times more investment in the latter period (see table A-10, Appendix A). There are several reasons for this marked increase in the ICOR. The rise in the share of infrastructure and the decline in the share of the very productive oil sector in total investment are two important causes of the higher ICOR. In addition, in the oil boom era of post-1973, Saudi Arabia has become a high-wage country and, therefore, investment projects have become more capital intensive. Greater capital intensity of investment also implies a higher ICOR. Finally, the limitation of absorptive capacity also causes an increase in ICOR. Nevertheless, the above economic factors are not totally responsible for the rise of ICOR in Saudi Arabia. Excessive investment in construction and the existence of waste and inefficiency in implementation of investment projects may also be important reasons for the higher ICOR. One example of the extravagance in construction spending is the new King Abdul Aziz International Airport near Jidda, which was built at a cost of about six billion dollars.[7] It is the world's largest airport, as large as Kennedy, LaGuardia, Newark, Chicago O'Hare, and Los Angeles airports combined.[8] There is a large body of informal evidence about the existence of considerable waste, inefficiency, and corruption in both development and nondevelopment expenditures. For example, many of the newly built industries suffer from excess capacity.[9] Reasons for this range from the generous loans provided to privileged businessmen by the Saudi Industrial Development Fund (SIDF) to inadequate planning by the few well-connected families who are overburdened by a large number of highly profitable projects.

DISTRIBUTION OF INCOME

When Saudi Arabia was a poor country, before the oil boom, the distribution of income was remarkably even.

The field survey by Motoko Katakura, an anthropologist who conducted her research from 1968 to 1970 in Wadi Fatima, western Saudi Arabia, provides valuable information about income distribution in the traditional Saudi communities. In the village of Bushur, where forty-six Bedouin families lived in 1970, the ratio of the highest to the lowest family income was sixteen. If the sheik of the village and the two teachers are excluded, the ratio of the highest to the lowest family income was only four (table 19).[10] In contrast to Bedouin communities, the gap between the lowest and the highest incomes in urban areas is substantially larger. In 1976, among those urban groups for which salary data are available, the ratio of the highest income to the lowest was thirty-one (table 19). If we had data on the highest salaries and profits, the income variance in the cities could be shown to be much larger. For example, a divisional manager working for a major construction contractor received an annual bonus of more than SR 1 million in 1978,[11] and the profit income of an influential middleman was more than $500 million between 1971 and 1977.[12] The degree of income inequality in urban areas can also be ascertained by an examination of the pattern of demand in the kingdom. A business guide to Saudi Arabia characterizes its consumer market as follows: "All markets in Saudi Arabia are [characterized by] good sales at the top and bottom of the line with relatively little movement of medium range goods. Very inexpensive items and luxury goods move best in most lines in Saudi Arabia."[13]

The difference between income distribution in urban and rural areas is noteworthy because it shows that urbanization can automatically increase the degree of political volatility in the kingdom. The poverty of a Bedouin living in a homogenous and egalitarian community was clearly tolerable since all his neighbors were equally poor. Now that he has moved to the highly differentiated and un-

TABLE 19

The Gap between the Lowest and Highest Incomes,
Rural Areas in 1970 and Urban Areas in 1976

| | Bedouin Village Bushur in 1970[a] Family Income: SR Per Month | | | Urban Areas: Wage Rate in 1976 SR Per Month | |
	All Households	Excluding the Sheik	Excluding Two Teachers and the Sheik	Including Expatriates	Excluding Expatriates
Income Receiver					
Lowest	60[b]	60[b]	60[b]	800[f]	800[f]
Highest	980[c]	560[d]	240[e]	25,000[g]	21,000[h]
Ratio of highest to lowest	16	9	4	31	26

SOURCES: Katakura, *Bedouin Village*, p. 116; Shilling, *Doing Business in Saudi Arabia*, p. 113.

[a] Excludes unemployed villagers
[b] A farmer
[c] The village sheik
[d] A teacher
[e] A laborer
[f] A Farash (errand boy, watchman, etc.)
[g] A middle-level executive (Western expatriate)
[h] A middle-level executive (Arab)

equal city, low income can cause considerable frustration and discontent.

The most important causes of the unequal distribution of income in urban areas are unequal endowments of skills and capital and unequal access to centers of political power. The latter factor is especially important because of the personalistic nature of decision making in the kingdom and the substantial share of the state in the national income. The wage differential is, to a great extent, caused by differences in endowments of skill and know-how, and it is likely to become smaller with the diffusion of education among the population.

Another source of income inequality in urban areas is the large difference between endowments of capital. As was discussed earlier, the Saudi business community is crowded with a large number of very small producers and traders. In 1976, among 77,301 business establishments, the number of medium-sized firms was less than 3,000 (table 14).[14] Although large firms are few, their share of private-sector capital is substantial. This can be seen from the data on manufacturing establishments for 1975. In that year, only 435 large establishments controlled 84 percent of industrial assets. The average value of assets in these units was more than one-hundred times that in establishments employing fewer than ten workers (table 20). The gap between the profit incomes of small and large business is also very wide. If we assume that the share of profits in value added is constant with respect to the size of firms, a comparison of the value added in small and large establishments can provide some indication of the size of this gap. In 1975, average value added in industrial establishments employing ten or more workers was forty times that in units employing fewer than ten workers (table 20). This greatly underestimates the variance of the profit incomes for the following reasons. First, instead of comparing the smallest with the

TABLE 20

Wealth and Income in the Private Manufacturing Sector, 1975

Employees Per Establishment	Number of Establishments	Fixed Assets		Value Added (At 1970 Prices)	
		Million SR	Per Establishment Thousand SR	Million SR	Per Establishment Thousand SR
1–9	9,500	167	17.6	260	27.4
10 and more	435	864	1,986.2	462	1,062.1
Total	9,935	1,031	103.8	722	72.7

SOURCE: K.O.S.A., Industrial Studies and Development Center, *Industrial Structure and Development in Saudi Arabia* (Riyadh: Industrial Studies and Development Center, 1977), table 3.1.

largest, we have compared the average small firm with the average large firm. Second, because large firms in the industrial sector are more capital intensive than the small firms, profits make up a large share of their value added. Finally, by comparing firms in one sector, we are ignoring the differences in profitability among sectors. This last factor is especially worthy of notice in Saudi Arabia since the super profits in the kingdom are not made in industry but in construction and trade.

Although the required data for a direct examination of the change in income distribution are not available, based on existing information it is possible to arrive at the following tentative conclusions. During the post-1973 oil-boom era, absolute poverty has been significantly reduced, and the relative income of the urban poor has not declined. However, the relative economic position of the urban middle-income groups has deteriorated while that of the very rich has improved. In short, the upper income groups have gained mainly at the expense of the middle-income population.

The Saudi state has used some of its enormous oil revenues to provide subsidies and relief payments for the low-income segment of the society. Stipendiary pensions are paid to the old, the permanently disabled, orphans, and single women without means of support. In addition, grants-in-aid are provided to persons who cannot work because of temporary disability, to those whose incomes have been affected by natural disaster, and to families of prisoners. Grants are also disbursed to low-income persons wishing to establish small businesses, and to the handicapped for the purchase of prostheses and medical aids. In 1980, the head of a family could receive SR 1,620, and each dependent SR 1,080 per year in the form of stipendiary pensions. The maximum for a family was SR 8,000 per year. Nearly 723,000 persons benefited from these pensions

in 1980.[15] In addition, 123,000 persons received temporary
relief assistance with an average value of SR 1,000 per person. These grants were mainly for consumption purposes.
Only 96 persons received grants for productive projects.
The average value of these payments was SR 1,600 per
person.[16]

In addition to direct subsidies, the state has also provided support for the poor through a number of other
schemes. In rural areas where the low productivity of peasants and nomads is a major cause of poverty, the government has provided farmers and livestock breeders interest-
free loans through the Saudi Arabian Agricultural Bank.
The bank, which was founded in 1964, had granted about
16,000 loans a year to the agricultural sector with an average value of SR 9,000 per loan by 1975. During the Second
Development Plan, the number of loans increased to 24,000
per year and their average value reached SR 30,000.[17] According to some observers, most peasants and nomads consider these loans as income and use a major portion of
them for consumption purposes.[18] Finally, subsidization
of inputs, and price supports for outputs have also been
used to enhance the income of the rural population. Some
of these incentives are summarized in table 21.

In urban areas the Saudi Credit Bank (SCB) provides
interest-free loans to persons with limited incomes for such
diverse purposes as marriage, home improvement, and establishment of workshops.[19] In addition, the Real Estate
Development Fund gives loans amounting to as much as 70
percent of the construction cost for owner-occupied resi-
dential units. Any Saudi male over twenty-one can ap-
ply for these loans. A married Saudi male can obtain a
loan at the age of eighteen. The credit extended to owner-
occupants includes a sizable subsidy element. A discount of
20 percent is provided for prompt payment of installments
and an additional 10 percent discount is added for one

TABLE 21

Government Incentives for Agricultural Production

Type of Incentive	Amount
Production input	
Fertilizer	50% of cost
Animal feed	50% of cost
Potato seed	5 tons free; thereafter, SR 1,000 per ton up to 15 tons
Machinery and equipment	
Poultry equipment	30% of cost
Dairy equipment	30% of cost
Engines and pumps	50% of cost
Fish trawlers	Variable
Transportation	
Air transport of cows	100% of cost
Output	
Wheat	SR 3.50 per kg[a]
Rice	SR 0.30 per kg
Corn	SR 0.25 per kg
Millet/barley	SR 0.15 per kg
Dates	SR 0.25 per kg
Date palms planted	SR 50.00 per tree

SOURCE: K.O.S.A., *Third Development Plan*, p. 143.

[a] Purchase price (1978–79).

lump-sum repayment. Between 1975 and 1980, the Real Estate Development Fund disbursed more than 150,000 loans for the construction of owner-occupied houses. The average value of these loans was SR 200,000.[20] Finally, it should be mentioned that the increased availability of free health services and the government's subsidization of essential commodities have also enhanced the welfare of the low-income segment of the society.[21]

Our conclusion about the relative income of the urban poor is based on data presented in table 22. In 1980, the wage rate for production labor was about twelve times

that of 1968. During the same period, per capita non-oil
GDP, which can be used as an index of average income in
the private sector, increased fourteenfold. Therefore, it is
possible to assert that during the period under consideration, the relative income of an urban wage earner remained
more or less unchanged. Of course, in absolute terms, the
real income of the urban working class has increased substantially since wage increases have been far greater than
the rise in the cost-of-living index (see table 22).

TABLE 22

Income of Production Workers and
Public Sector Employees, 1968 and 1980

	1968 (a)	1980 (b)	a/b
Wage income of production workers (SR per day)[a]	8	100	12.5
Index of public sector salaries (1968 = 100)[b]	100	730	7.3
Non-oil GDP per capita (SR per year)[c]	1,110	15,760	14.2
Consumer price index (1975 = 100)	46.5	152.4	3.3

SOURCES: Tables A-1, A-3, A-4, Appendix A; K.O.S.A., *Statistical
Indicators 1980*, p. 49; K.O.S.A., *Statistical Yearbook 1980*, p. 501;
IMF, *International Financial Statistics 1982*, p. 391; United Nations,
Studies on Development Problems of Countries of Western Asia 1974
(New York: United Nations, 1975), p. 91.

[a] Assumes 24 working days per month.
[b] Implicit deflator of value added in public services.
[c] At current factor prices, based on the revised price system.

The major middle-income groups in urban areas are
government employees and owners of small- and medium-
sized firms. Both these groups seem to have experienced
a decline in relative income. From 1968 to 1980, the salary
of government employees, unlike the income of production workers, did not keep up with the rise in per capita

non-oil GDP (table 22).[22] The slower rise of public-sector salaries compared to the wages of unskilled workers indicates a narrowing of the income gap between the lower- and middle-income groups in urban areas. This is probably caused by the increasing supply of educated manpower and the gradual disappearance of the quasi-rent received by the few who had access to educational opportunities before the oil boom of the 1970s. However, this narrowing gap does not necessarily imply a reduction of social tension. In fact, it may cause considerable frustration among the educated entrants of the labor market. Those lower-income people who have gone to school with expectations of joining the affluent middle class may become disillusioned as they find out that the relative income gain that comes from higher education is not as great as it used to be. Since the state is the major employer of the educated work force, it will eventually be blamed for the decline in the relative income of this class. This resentment will be especially intensified if government employees consider the state's nonwage expenditures wasteful and extravagant.

Two major causes of the decline in the relative income of the urban middle-income entrepreneurs and the rise in that of urban big business, are inflation and government policy. During the years from 1970 to 1980, the prices in the construction sector increased more than eightfold while those in industry and services tripled and quadrupled, respectively (table 23). Consequently, investors in the construction sector received enormous windfall profits. In industry and services the producers have had to increase productivity and output at a much faster rate in order to keep their profits at levels comparable to those of investors in the construction sector. This may have been easy for the large and modern producers. But for small and traditional producers and traders, growth of productivity is usually low, and their ability to expand output is

TABLE 23

Prices in Urban Sectors, 1980
(*Excluding petroleum production and refining*)

Sector	Value Added Deflator (1970 = 1)
Industry[a]	3.3
Construction	8.4
Private services[b]	4.4

SOURCES: Tables A-3, A-4, Appendix A.

[a] Includes mining, manufacturing, and utilities.

[b] Includes trade, transportation, communications, storage, finance, insurance, real estate, business services, and community, social, and personal services.

quite limited because of inadequate access to credit and new techniques and competition from large and modern businesses. Furthermore, since most of the largest private firms are in the construction industry, it is reasonable to conclude that as a result of inflation, the gap has increased considerably between the incomes of small- and medium-sized manufacturers, and service establishments on the one hand, and the large construction companies on the other.

Another cause of growing inequality in the business community has been government policy. To encourage investment, the state has provided generous subsidies and incentives to private business. But the main beneficiaries have been the big firms. For example in industry, the Saudi Industrial Development Fund provides interest-free loans for up to 50 percent of the capital requirements of projects in the manufacturing sector.[23] For electric utility projects, the fund supplies up to 100 percent of the investment requirements.[24] Between 1975 and 1979, the loans disbursed by SIDF exceeded SR 16 billion.[25] In 1977, the credit supplied by the fund made up about one-half of all investments by the private sector in non-oil manufacturing projects.[26] However, the Saudi Industrial Development Fund has mainly served the big industrialists. It finances only those projects that are licensed by the Ministry of Industry and Electricity.[27] These tend to be large in terms of invested capital, employment, and production capacity.[28] Between 1975 and 1979, the average size of industrial loans granted by SIDF was SR 12.3 million.[29]

The only government institution that provides credit to small urban enterprises is the Saudi Credit Bank. However, the financial resources of this bank are extremely limited and most of its loans are consumption oriented. Between 1975 and 1979, loans supplied by the Saudi Credit Bank were less than 3 percent of those disbursed by the Saudi Industrial Development Fund.[30] During 1976–80, only 2 percent of the credit granted by the Saudi Credit Bank was for productive purposes (table 24). The av-

TABLE 24

Loans Granted by the
Saudi Credit Bank, 1976–80

Purpose	Number of Loans	Value SR Thousand	Percentages of Total
Marriage	35,621	175.1	40.3
House construction	33,644	249.6	57.5
Occupation	557	9.3	2.2
Medical treatment	27	2.0	0
Total	69,849	434.2	100.0

SOURCE: K.O.S.A., *Statistical Yearbook 1980*, p. 464.

erage value of these loans was only SR 17,000. Other incentives provided by government to the private sector are also biased in favor of big business. Nominal fees for land in industrial parks, import tax exemptions for industrial equipment and raw materials, low utility rates, preferential treatment in government purchases, technical assistance, market information, and other privileges are granted only to those industrial enterprises holding a government license.[31] In 1978, of more than 13,000 private establishments in the industrial sector, only 687 were licensed by the Ministry of Industry and Electricity, and therefore, could benefit from the government's generous incentives and subsidies.[32]

6

The Erosion of Authority

The contemporary Saudi state plays a more prominent role in the direction of the economy than its own immediate antecedents, or most Western countries. The control of the economy endows the state with the ability to exert extensive control over the society. At the same time, the political ramifications arising out of economic problems have centered on the state leadership. The identification of the state with the royal family makes it even easier to trace the sources of economic maladjustments to actual individuals. The absence of political abstraction, rules, and procedures, and the dominance of personalities, relations, and discretion, help to bring into focus objects for political opposition. These objects are imbued with a quality of reality that gives rise to intense emotions in the masses, which ultimately lead to violent political action. Consequently, economic bottlenecks, shortages, unequal distribution of income, inflation, and declining purchasing power are not problems for which responsibility can be divided among history, society, or circumstances. Rather, they are the problems of the state and are particularly attributable to the main decision makers within the state. When miseries exist, which are deemed unnecessary, and their perpetrators are identified, men can be expected to rebel.

The rapid change in the class structure of Saudi Arabia, the high rate of urbanization, and expansion of communication patterns, all brought about by the economic activities of the state, have had a serious impact on the universalization of values in the Saudi society. Differences, social as well as economic, which were tolerated in the segmented Arabian society of the past as God made, have deepened and widened at a time when more and more Saudis define these differences as social creations and consider them immoral. The state, as the vehicle for the royal family's rule, is easily identified as the creator of artificial and unjust differences.

The burden on the state to meet the new challenges of a rapidly modernizing society is a serious one. The state can be credited with the creation and internal cohesion of Saudi society; but as an external force, it is still weak. The men who fill its rank-and-file are often dissatisfied. Their relative income is declining as is their social status. In the face of sustained political opposition, the state institutions will probably crumble from within.

The present regime in Saudi Arabia has failed to develop viable institutional supports. The traditional mores, at the same time, have weakened as the money economy has expanded to include the whole nation. The early rule of the Saudi family was facilitated partly by the fragmentation of Arabian society and economy. As the premodern divisions of the society are gradually being replaced by a sense of nationhood, political demands are bound to increase. Conflict over the distribution of wealth, power, and status by the central authorities will develop far beyond anything experienced in the past.

The study of Arabia's political development clearly indicates that from its inception the state has been unable to mobilize support, and instead, has depended on fragmentation and neutralization of potential opposition. Any power center is perceived as potentially dangerous, and this includes the state's own institutions. The military, the bureaucracy, and the religious institutions are arranged in such a way that they are internally immobilized. Deprived of internal bases of support, the regime has become overly dependent on external support, particularly on that of the United States. Dependence will, in turn, affect the regime's legitimacy to the detriment of both the Saudis and the United States.

CORRUPTION

The pervasive corruption that exists in government and business is seriously affecting the regime's legitimacy and has fostered political opposition. To many Western observers of the Saudi government, corruption is simply a Western value term for the manner in which Middle Easterners have done business for generations; and consequently, they downplay the destabilizing effect of corruption. Unethical practices such as family aggrandizement, conflict of interests, and bribery are presumably acceptable to Middle Easterners.[1] One scholar has gone so far as to argue that "'corruption' often exists in the eye of the beholder," and went on to say that what is considered in Western cultural perspective as corrupt, is acceptable to the Islamic concept of justice and tradition of Bedouin sharing.[2] An intelligence report by the Central Intelligence Agency argued in the same vein that "since personal enrichment is accepted by everyone, beginning with the royal family, as one of the prerogatives of public office, acceptance of bribes and speculation of public funds are common."[3]

Some of the corruption is indeed related to the mores of patrimonialism in which the state is conceived as the

property of the prince's family, and where there is little dif-
ferentiation between public funds and private purse. But
the prince, in turn, was perceived as the father of his people, and his benevolence was based on the fairness with
which he distributed material and abstract goods among
his subjects. The sheik of the tribe was not much richer
than his men and his life-style was not that different from
theirs. Avaricious rulers were held in contempt and often
lost their legitimacy and their rule. The past cannot be
resurrected to justify the present degree of corruption and
financial empires that are being built. Nor can one argue
that the social structure that supported the value system
of the past is still maintained. At any rate, even if the society had remained the same, it would not have legitimized
the extent of corruption that exists today. The enormous
increase in revenues accruing to the rulers affects the stan-
dards by which such acts are judged. In contemporary
Saudi Arabian ruling structure, norms are lost and limits
have disappeared. Social groups, however, are becoming
increasingly critical of the way the state finances are being handled. Given that the royal family has depended on
a diffuse sense of legitimacy rather than a concentrated
base of support such as a party or a bureaucracy, its loss
of legitimacy is even more destabilizing than it would be
in other regimes that have solid, organized support.

Large-scale corruption and mismanagement began with
King 'Abd al-'Aziz, the founder of the modern Saudi state.
St. John Philby, the king's closest adviser for thirty years,
estimated that of over $1.25 billion in revenues received by
the state between 1946 and 1953, a mere $90 million was
spent on public projects.[4] Corruption of this proportion
(then as now) was an outgrowth of increasing interaction
with the West.

Western companies that make illegal pay-offs, generally justify their conduct as the necessary way of doing

business in what they consider the amoral business atmosphere of the Middle East. Agents' fees of 20 to 30 percent on company-to-government sales, which are then used to bribe officials, have been common. In light of the total value of the sales, agents' fees, which often only buy influence, are indeed enormous. According to the testimony of James Akins, the U.S. ambassador to Saudi Arabia, Saudi officials were under the impression that no fees were paid on government-to-government sales. To their apparent surprise, they discovered fees of up to $70 million being paid in military sales between governments. The Saudis issued a decree forbidding all agents' fees on government-to-government sales and limiting all other fees to a flat 5 percent.[5] In spite of the Saudi government's apparent clamp down and the assurances of the U.S. government that no fees were being paid, the Northrop Corporation explicitly authorized its agent, Adnan Khashoggi to pay $450,000 to two Saudi military officials to expedite a sale of F-15s. In fact, in the course of Senate hearings on the matter, T. V. Jones, chairman of the Northrop Corporation, implied that he was assured by certain officials in the U.S. government that the restrictions on payments were removed.[6] When Senator Charles Percy inquired as to U.S. complicity in the bribes, the following exchange took place:

> Senator Percy: To your knowledge, did the government at that time have knowledge that there were agents' fees?
> Ambassador Akins: Our government?
> Percy: Yes.
> Akins: Of course.[7]

Contrary to this information, Ambassador Akins had assured Prince Sultan, the minister of defense and aviation, and his deputy, Prince Turki, that no agents' fees were paid, and that Northrop did not have an agent in the country, on the technicality that Khashoggi had con-

veniently arranged to be abroad at the time.[8] In fact, in
the same period, an American defense contractor paid over
$300 million to two Saudi officials.[9] The present state of
corruption in Saudi Arabia must be analyzed in the context of the desire of foreign companies to reap huge profits
(sometimes as high as 600 percent). To amass these fortunes, foreign businessmen are willing to pay bribes, which
they can rationalize as the Middle Eastern way of doing
business.[10]

Nonetheless, it is not only foreign firms that have vi-
tiated the Saudi social structure (although without their
full and willing participation, such enormous corruption
would not have been possible). The nature of Saudi rule
has much to do with the extent of corruption. Despite
pious expressions by the Saudi government, the state is
formed as a family corporation to enrich the royal household and those who serve the household. The state is
farmed out in the form of monopolies. King Fahd's son
Prince Muhammad, had the spot-market oil concession
during the oil shortage of 1980-81. His one-man opera-
tion, Petromonde, showed a profit of about $11 million a
month. The eldest of the royal clan, Prince Muhammad
ibn 'Abd al-'Aziz (the enraged grandfather in the "death
of a princess" tragedy) was allotted 500,000 barrels of oil
a day to dispose of at will.[11] Such cases as these are not
only detrimental to the economic well-being of Saudi Arabia, but are bound to create havoc in the international
oil market. Apparently others including Zaki Yamani, the
minister of oil and Ghaith Far'un, a Saudi businessman
with close contacts to the royal household, are involved in
making profitable oil agreements, which at times earn up
to $100 million a day.[12]

Some economic plans are especially designed for corrupt practices. Unnecessary and major projects guarantee
a steady flow of capital. The new airport at Jidda and

the King Khalid Military City are only the most blatant examples. As the construction boom fed by oil revenues is spiraling upward, multibillion dollar profits are being made in land speculation. Desert land is often bought at a low price and sold to the government for large construction projects. One prince reportedly made a $2 billion profit on the sale of the land on which the Jubail industrial complex is being built.[13] The desire for personal aggrandizement contradicts the generalized goals of economic development. Contractors are at times encouraged to double their bids and split the mark-up with the officials who grant the concession. Apparently as much as $200 million in an $800 million contract for the purchase of British Lightning Fighters consisted of commissions.[14]

POLITICAL OPPOSITION

The Saudi record on human rights, while lamentable, is not as tragic as those of many other Middle Eastern countries.[15] Nor is the livelihood of an average citizen as meager as those in some neighboring states. Political freedom does not exist in the country, but it does not exist in other comparable states either. Yet, under conditions that many would find satisfactory, the Saudi society is marked by apathy, alienation, and political opposition to the system of government. In fact, as early as the mid-fifties a U.S. intelligence report observed that King Saud's government, through "a combination of force, intimidation, and bribery," had led the country to social disorder. The report predicted, "Eventually, these now fragmented dissident elements may find common cause and engage in assassination and terrorism as a prelude to complete overthrow of the regime."[16]

Some of the opposition can be related to the nature of the familial state, which has increasingly become anachronistic in view of rapid social change. Acceptance of a government's legitimacy, which is merely a family monopoly, is not easily tolerated by an urbanite whose primordial attachments are being replaced by a sense of class awareness. The corruption of the regime has further put its legitimacy into question. The contemporary Saudi subject believes that his national treasury is being depleted through an alliance of multinational corporations and the royal family; and in the process his country has become dependent on the multinationals and their home countries. The dissatisfaction with political and economic decision making has brought about three categories of political opposition: (1) that generated within the state organizations and the ruling family itself; (2) the leftist and nationalist movements with more radical goals; and (3) the recent politico-religious movements, which have actively sought the transformation of the state. A U.S. intelligence report compiled in 1956 found the military establishment as potentially the most dangerous group challenging the stability of the government. As early as April 1955, senior officers had conspired to assassinate King Saud and Premier Faisal in order to establish a military government similar to President Nasir's government in Egypt. Betrayed by an informer, the conspirators were all executed.[17] In 1963, during the outbreak of the Yemeni civil war, nine pilots defected to Egypt. In 1969, a group of air force officers were arrested for conspiring against the state. Their attempted coup, inspired by Nasir's charismatic appeal and supported by some left-wing teachers and Aramco workers was again discovered only a few hours before it was to take place. In both cases those arrested were brutally dealt with.[18]

A second coup attempt in 1969 was organized by the Hejazi bourgeoisie and other reformist elements who were promised fundamental changes by Faisal before his accession to the throne. Disappointed with Faisal, but supported by some senior Saudi officers, including retired general 'Abd Allah Aysi and 'Ali Zain al-Abidin, they staged an unsuccessful coup.[19] The organizers of the second coup were associated at one point with a dissatisfied group within the royal household itself, known as the "liberal princes."

Nine princes pushed for reform in 1958. Four of them were finally forced to seek refuge with President Nasir, the archenemy of Saudi royalty. One of them, Prince Talal, the king's younger brother, repeatedly broadcast on Radio Cairo, exhorting his countrymen to rebel against his reigning brother.[20] The solidarity of the Saudi clan has never been as firm as it is presumed. Historically, they have conspired, and even murdered each other. In 1975, King Faisal was assassinated by his own nephew, Prince Faisal ibn Musa'id. Almost ten years earlier, the prince's brother, Khalid, was killed while protesting against such innovations by King Faisal as the introduction of television, which he found to be corrupting the moral fabric of the Saudi society.

The royal clan is held together by external dangers to them all, rather than by intrinsic bonds among them. Divided into subgroups, they vie for power among themselves. Clusters of full brothers are positioned against half brothers. The most prominent example is the present conflict between King Fahd and his half-brother and crown-prince, 'Abd Allah.[21] Within this byzantine mosaic of intrigues and conflicts, there is at times, opposition to the nature of the rulership itself.

A more serious opposition to the system, however, consists of secular forces, which include both the nationalist groups as well as the left. The nationalists are either outside the hierarchy of rulership, or are on the fringes of the system. Within the bureaucracy there are certain politi-

cized elements who would like to see the clannish auto-
cratic regime change to a democratic form of government.
They share their sentiments with many Hejazi families who
are still not comfortable with the Nejdi domination of the
society.

More dangerous to the regime are leftist and working-
class movements whose histories go back to the summer
of 1953. The Saudi workers of Aramco went on strike
for two weeks demanding pay increases and an end to
discrimination (particularly in housing) between them and
their American counterparts. It is generally accepted that
the strike was widespread and was supported by all Saudi
workers.[22] The Workers' Committee, which was formed
during the strike, remained active though clandestine until
it was repressed after the 1956 strikes, which it led, were
broken. The members of the committee, reflecting upon
the lessons of the strikes, drew different conclusions. Many
felt that the moderate politics of trade unionism were not
applicable to Saudi Arabia. As a result these members
went on to form the nuclei of more radical and purely
political organizations.

Between the two strikes, the oil fields were not quiet.
In 1955, about one hundred Palestinians were arrested and
deported in a midnight roundup. Many others were arrested on the grounds that they were communists.[23] In
spite of repressions, serious demonstrations broke out in
1956 when, in the presence of the king himself, thousands
of workers in Dahran demonstrated and held banners read-
ing, "We want an elected trade union," and "Down with
American imperialism."[24]

Former members of the Workers' Committee, in conjunction with communists, formed the National Reform
Front in 1956. The front was inherently immobilized because of the conflict between its moderate and radical
wings. Finally the communists broke away and formed the

National Liberation Front (NLF) in 1958. The NLF, which ideologically follows the Soviet Union, is the closest equivalent to a Saudi Arabian Communist party. Not a powerful or popular organization, nevertheless it participated in the attempted coup of 1969.[25]

The mid-fifties to the mid-sixties was an era of Arab nationalism under the influence of President Nasir's charismatic appeal. Throughout this period, the radical forces on the left, such as the communists; and the conservative forces, such as the remaining Arab monarchists, were on the defensive against the ad lib ideology of Arab socialism expounded in Cairo and advertised throughout the Arab world by Radio Cairo. It is not surprising that the most active organization in the sixties was the Union of People of the Arabian Peninsula (UPAP). A Nasirist organization, UPAP had strong support among the workers, the army, and even some of the tribes. It claimed responsibility for a number of bomb explosions, which in late 1966 shook the kingdom. During its heyday the UPAP, fueled by the patriotism generated by the October War, organized massive demonstrations in Qatif, Dammam, Khubar, Dahran, and Ra's al-Tanurah. Oil production completely stopped.[26]

As is characteristic of many opposition groups in Saudi Arabia, the UPAP has not published a program and its reliance on Nasir's Egypt and the propaganda war waged by Radio Cairo proved to be a serious mistake. The debacle of the October War in 1967 and the discredit that it brought to Nasir undermined the UPAP's organization and its appeal. Gradually Egypt, instead of advocating change, came to depend on the financial resources of the conservative Arab regimes, particularly Saudi Arabia.

In 1969 when the impact of the Arab defeat was fully realized, mass arrests of the UPAP's members sealed the fate of the already weakened organization. While it still exists, support for the UPAP is limited to some members

of the regular armed forces and the Shammar tribe in the
north, which historically has opposed the Saudi regime.[27]

The perception of subjugation to foreign rule and dis-
gust at the high level of corruption have manifested themselves in puritanical and often atavistic and chauvinistic
movements, which shook the kingdom, most strikingly in
1979. It is often stated that the ulema and the state, in
contrast to the Shah's Iran, maintain close relationship.
Yet, the religious opposition to the state has frequently not
come from the establishment ulema, but from the marginal
elements whose politically motivated mission has the cer-
tainty and the purity of religion. In these situations the
traditional religion and the traditional ruling class are both
opposed.

Juhaiman ibn Muhammad (the leader of the group
that seized the Great Mosque on November 20, 1979) published a pamphlet in 1978 in which he declared that the
ulema were bought off by the royal family and were equally
corrupt. He denounced Shaikh 'Abd al-'Aziz ibn Baz, the
blind chief theologian of the holy city of Medina, as a man
who knew his theology and jurisprudence but had put his
knowledge at the service of the regime.[28] Given the absence of a church structure, the authority of the Muslim
cleric depends on the relationship he maintains with the
masses. Association of the ulema with the state, therefore,
may damage the ulema's popularity, but not necessarily
grant the state religious acceptability.

From all indications it appears that there is a surge
of a new religious consciousness. In contrast to the traditional religion, symbolized by the ulema, which has become passive and apolitical, the new religiosity is active,
and its religious demonology is applied to political life. The
morality of religion is brought into daily life; and consequently, the compromises with the regime that the ulema
have traditionally contracted are deemed sinful.

In 1979, there were general disturbances at the religious college in the holy city of Medina. The religious
college of Mahd al-Da'wah at Mecca was in turmoil during the same period, and students at the University of
Riyadh went on a rampage expressing their contempt for
the regime's lax sense of morality. A young student from
the University of Riyadh, calling himself Shaikh Ahmad
is still active, leading a band of students, requiring proof
from married couples, and punishing anyone wearing jew-
elry or whose hair is not fully covered.[29]

Many of these personalities are indirectly unleashed by
the regime itself. Shaikh Ahmad is a *matawwah,* a func-
tionary of the OPGDE. Juhaiman was a member of the
National Guard who was influenced by the orthodox theo-
logical teachings of ibn Baz but decided to give his religious findings political meaning. The religious college in
the city of Medina, where the riots of 1979 were concentrated, was established with the help of the government
in the hope of combating the ideas of Arab socialism em-
anating from Cairo. The revolt of Juhaiman took place
after Prince Na'if, the minister of interior, had issued a
number of religiously inspired edicts that banned women
from traveling alone and working with men. A dress code,
also, was promised by the minister.[30]

Unable to offer a rival ideology, the regime is reduced
to an apologist. Its conservative and traditional nature
compels it to ally itself with religious formations and sentiments. The ostentatious life-style of its elite casts it in
an immoral and hypocritical light. Its continuous protes-
tations over its religiosity further accentuate its image of
weakness and deception. Consequently, the regime is continuously on the defensive. It is not able to challenge religious thought, take initiatives, or offer alternatives.

In the process of urbanization, the mosques fill up.
The detribalized city dweller looks to religion as a cultural

map to guide him through the unfamiliar and expanding city. The formerly passive symbols of religion are reinterpreted to suit the new social environment. Much of this process will take place within the traditional religious establishment (just as it did in Iran) before it supersedes and eventually discards traditional religion.

The most dramatic case in point was the capture of the holiest shrine of Islam, the mosque in Mecca, on November 20, 1979, a date that coincided with the onset of the fifteenth Islamic century, and a day of eschatological significance.[31] The guerrillas who took over the mosque could not have been as few as the government announced–around 200. The mosque, which sprawls over forty-six acres, has a central courtyard that can accommodate 300,000 worshipers. At the time of the take-over, there were between 40,000 and 50,000 worshipers present. It seems highly unlikely that 200 guerrillas would be able to control the entire area. The fact that it took two weeks for goverment forces to recapture the mosque at a casualty cost of 427 officers and troops is a further indication that the number of guerrillas was probably deliberately underestimated.

There were other religious demonstrations at the same time. The Shi'ites of al-Hasa fought the National Guard from 25 November to the thirtieth. The oil producing eastern provinces of the kingdom seemed seriously endangered for a week. Medina was the scene of scattered riots and arrests that were connected with the Mecca episode.[32] In the face of general disturbances, it is difficult to accept the government's claims that Juhaiman's rebellion was the isolated act of a few deranged and religiously misguided individuals. In fact, they may have represented only a small fraction of the populace who harbored similar sentiments. If a few hundred men are willing to go on a suicide mission, one may only speculate on the number who are willing to oppose the system, albeit less dramatically.

It is equally significant that in contrast to the government's claims, the ideology and goals of the rebels in Mecca was fundamentally political. They believed that the Saudi leadership, both sacred and secular, had forfeited its duty to defend an Islamic land against corruption and foreign domination. The rule of the *mahdi,* which was proposed as an alternative to the Saudi royal family should not be confused with the infallible and Messianic meanings that the Shi'ites ascribe to. Rather, to Juhaiman, as to the Sunni tradition, the *mahdi* is a leader who symbolizes the aspirations of his people and is morally qualified to rule. The writings of Juhaiman are not as concerned with theology as they are with the question of political rulership.[33] And the demands made during the seizure of the mosque were entirely political.[34]

A former, unidentified Saudi ambassador, who had a long history of service to his country, told the *New York Times* that the Mecca incident was long overdue. "There is," he said, "spreading feeling of unrest and impatience with the uneven justice, with the huge commissions paid to princes, with the double standard we have to live with." The diplomat went on to say that "the people in Mecca were asking for a change in the ruling system. They were saying that the royalty is non-Islamic. Even if I do not agree with that, I tell you this movement is much bigger than its leadership suggest."[35]

The mosque incident was particularly menacing to the regime because of the reports that some of the rebels were members of the National Guard.[36] While the government denied that more than one rebel was a member of the National Guard, in the light of earlier unrest in the military, it would not be surprising if some of the guerrillas had received their training within the National Guard and their heavy arms from its armories.

Conclusion

Until the re-emergence of the Saudis in the first quarter of the twentieth century, Arabia was not a unified society. Various types of economies: trade in Hejaz, fishing and pearl diving in the Gulf areas, nomadism in Nejd, and agriculture in the southwest constituted the basis of different social structures that had little in common. The integration of Arabia as a consequence of political centralization under the Saudi family, and value integration under the impact of puritanical Islam, that is, Wahhabism, is a contemporary situation and poses new problems. Integration of the society has been accelerated as oil has come to dominate all aspects of the economy, reducing the former major economic activities to the periphery, and thus laying the foundations of a more tightly integrated society than was possible earlier.

In the past twenty years, Saudi Arabia has been transformed into a highly urbanized society, and its urban population is now concentrated in the three cities of Riyadh, Jidda, and Mecca. While the majority of the Saudi population is still uneducated, this situation is not expected to last for long. The literacy rate and the population's level of education are both likely to rise very rapidly in the 1980s. The kingdom has changed from a society of nomads, farmers, and fishermen to one of urban workers employed by the government and small private firms. However, the ascendance of the urban working class is only a temporary phenomenon. By the middle of the 1990s, the kingdom is likely to be dominated by the rapidly growing professional middle class.

Since income distribution is far more unequal in the urban areas than in the rural areas, urbanization will automatically increase the degree of political volatility in Saudi society. The most important causes of income inequality in urban areas are unequal educational opportunities, differences in endowments of capital, and unequal access to the centers of political power. While the diffusion of education will rectify the first cause of inequality, the other two are not likely to disappear as easily. New policies and institutions are necessary to reduce their negative impact on income distribution.

One reason why the kingdom has enjoyed relative political stability in the post-1973 oil boom era may be that the income share of the working class has not declined. However, the increase in the income share of the high income urban group at the expense of the middle class may cause serious political problems. The size of the latter group will increase in the future and so will its ability to effect political change. In addition to urbanization, diffusion of education, and the changing class structure, other factors that are raising the public's political awareness and its material aspirations are extensive contacts with people from other cultures, mass communications, and mobility.

The state has so far failed to develop appropriate institutions to deal with the growing sense of nationhood. The traditional institutions cannot adequately bridge the gap between the emerging modern nation and its rulers.

Nor are they still viable in their traditional forms. The Islamic Brotherhoods were suppressed at their formative stage and the tribal social structure, which supported the Saudi family, has become politically insignificant as a result of the Saudi policies and exigencies of new economic and political realities.

The Saudi state has developed in response to the international setting, rather than out of the internal dynamics of the society. The historical development of Saudi Arabia in the past fifty years has further accentuated the dichotomy between the state and the society. As a result of the dramatic increase in oil revenues, the state is not dependent on the productive capabilities of its citizens for economic survival. While the external economic dependence of the state has increased as a result of the rapid growth of imports and the expatriate work force, the Saudi population has also become more dependent on the state as a consequence of the massive expansion of public-sector employment and the proliferation of various types of direct and indirect government subsidies.

The autonomy of the state from its citizens is, in the long run, destabilizing. Unable to mobilize the energies of its own population, the Saudi political system will remain weak and may collapse. Historically, the efforts of the state have been aimed at neutralizing potential threats rather than mobilizing their support. The state, in short, has so far depended on the fragmentation of the society but the society is becoming increasingly unified. Fearful of competing power groups and military coups, the state has not allowed its own institutions to develop any coherence.

The emergent bureaucratic structure is not systemized and rationalized; traditional mores persist. Official functions are conceived to be pieces of property. Administration is conducted from case to case. Officials have little authority to pursue the duties of their offices. Since the official areas of jurisdiction are not clear, little is accomplished, and yet, the rate of bureaucratic conflict remains very high. To correct the bureaucratic lethargy and inefficiency, new bureaus are established that will drain the regular bureaucracy of the few talented and able bureaucrats and create more intergovernmental conflict. A rationalized bureaucracy inherently threatens the interest of the privileged few, who find any kind of regularization a limitation of their own powers. The failure of the state to develop appropriate institutions, and the personalistic nature of decision making have caused incongruence between the priorities of the public and the actual allocation of resources, inefficiency and waste in the use of oil revenues, and the accumulation of massive wealth by a small segment of the population.

The military, like the bureaucracy, is fragmented and factionalized. The regular military units are incapable of a concerted action. The National Guard is completely independent of the regular army and, in fact, is set up as a rival force. And the small population of Saudi Arabia cannot support a large military force, at any rate.

As a consequence of internal weak links, and the inability of the state to satisfy the rising expectation of an increasingly integrated society, the state has to rely on external support. The maintenance of this outside support requires policies—sustaining a high level of oil production for instance—that will adversely affect the system's legitimacy and stability. The integration of Saudi Arabia in the world market system has generated an urban class structure that contradicts the patrimonial state. The contradiction between the society and the state will bring about, in the long run, political conflict and instability.

This study has traced the development of the state from a tribal sheikdom to a patrimonial monarchy as a consequence of integration in the world market system.

It is proposed that the increasing power of the state is paralleled by societal transformation from a tribal to a class society. Finally, the study has shown the emerging contradiction between the state and society.

Most studies on the Arab world have concentrated on the internal political development. A few have studied the political impact of the West. What is often neglected is the extent to which the Arab world has become part of the world system and the inevitable societal ramifications produced by this integration. Early specialization in cotton and oil production have made the Arabs dependent on the international market system. The rate of production is increasingly determined by international exigencies rather than domestic needs. This has also brought about the economic integration of the society to a degree that was unforseen two generations ago. Autonomous economies that existed independent of the state have either disappeared or have become subject to state regulations. The rapid socioeconomic change, resulting from the externality of the causes of change, has brought about uneven development. Precapitalist formations, capitalist relations, and etatism exist side by side, creating not only confusion but contradictions. The study of Saudi Arabia as a case, throws light on these problems, which are endemic to the Arab world.

During the embryonic period of the Saudi dynasty, Arabia was a segmental society in which the component parts were constantly shifting and regrouping. This society was held together by its inner conflict. In spite of tension and friction (in fact, because of it) the society tended toward equilibrium. The ruler's area of authority was limited. The discovery and exploitation of oil, and the subsequent integration of Saudi Arabia in the world system, has transformed the segmental system into a patrimonial one, where the state is perceived as the property of the ruling family. Major officials of the kingdom are the members of the ruler's household, and consequently, the bureaucracy has developed as the extension of the household. The state has become anthropomorphized as a family. As a consequence of uneven development, contradictions have multiplied. While the economic penetration of Arabia has transformed and strengthened the traditional family rule, it has also fostered the rise of a modern class structure. Economically, the ruling family and its servants have adopted modern middle-class behavior while politically, they continue to adhere to patrimonial mores.

TABLE A-1

Population of Saudi Arabia, 1952–80

Year	Mid-Year Population (*Millions*)	Year	Mid-Year Population (*Millions*)
1952	4.06	1967	5.70
1953	4.14	1968	5.86
1954	4.22	1969	6.03
1955	4.31	1970	6.20
1956	4.39	1971	6.38
1957	4.48	1972	6.57
1958	4.58	1973	6.76
1959	4.68	1974	6.97
1960	4.79	1975	7.18
1961	4.90	1976	7.40
1962	5.02	1977	7.63
1963	5.14	1978	7.87
1964	5.27	1979	8.11
1965	5.41	1980	8.37
1966	5.56		

SOURCES: United Nations, *Demographic Yearbook 1970*, p. 130., ibid., *1971*, p. 135; ibid., *1972*, p. 143; ibid.,*1973*, p. 104; ibid., *1974*, p. 130; ibid., *1975*, p. 163; ibid., *1976*, p. 140; ibid., *1977*, p. 161; ibid., *1978*, p. 118; ibid., *1979*, p. 180; ibid., *1980*, p. 155.

TABLE A-2
Selected Saudi Oil Statistics

Year	Production (*Million barrels*)	Posted Price[a,b] ($ *U.S. per barrel*)	Oil Revenues (*Million $ U.S.*)
1960	481.4	1.800	333.7
1961	540.5	–	377.6
1962	599.8	–	409.7
1963	651.7	–	607.3
1964	694.1	–	524.2
1965	804.9	–	664.1
1966	949.7	–	789.9
1967	1023.8	–	903.6
1968	1113.7	–	926.4
1969	1173.9	1.800	949.2
1970	1386.7	1.800	1,214.0
1971	1740.6	2.285	1,884.9
1972	2202.0	2.484	2,744.6
1973	2772.6	5.036	4,340.1
1974	3095.1	11.651	22,573.5
1975	2582.5	11.951	25,676.2
1976	3139.3	12.376	30,754.9
1977	3358.0	13.660	36,540.1
1978	3038.0	13.660	32,233.8
1979	3479.2	24.000[c]	48,435.2
1980	3623.8	32.000[c]	84,466.4

SOURCES: Saudi Arabian Monetary Agency (SAMA), *Annual Report 1975*, pp. 110–11; ibid., *1981*, pp. 138–39; K.O.S.A., *Statistical Yearbook 1978*, p. 257; ibid., *1979*, p. 286; ibid., *1980*, p. 310; Knauerhase, *The Saudi Arabian Economy*, p. 209; *Petroleum Economist*, December 1978, p. 539.

[a] Arabian light crude.
[b] The prevailing price on December 31 of each year.
[c] Government selling price.

TABLE A-3

Gross Domestic Product by Economic Activity
(At current factor prices: million Saudi riyals)

Sector	1967	1968	1969	1970	1971	1972	1973	1974	1975	1975ᵃ	1976ᵃ	1977ᵃ	1978ᵃ	1979ᵃ	1980ᵃ,ᵇ
Agriculture, forestry, fishing	846	881	957	984	1,016	1,059	1,139	1,242	1,392	1,392	1,586	1,866	3,909	4,196	4,648
Mining and quarrying															
Crude petroleum and natural gas	6,131	6,893	7,270	8,106	12,581	16,932	26,284	78,345	104,696	104,696	109,560	128,466	126,156	131,098	241,708
Others	36	44	49	47	50	59	90	146	248	264	535	823	1,025	1,120	1,341
Manufacturing															
Petroleum refining	760	902	985	1,241	1,474	1,442	1,811	4,347	5,766	5,766	5,962	6,221	5,908	7,442	10,276
Others	309	344	385	431	484	543	617	730	931	1,600	2,211	3,063	4,066	5,173	6,467
Electricity, gas, water	199	220	247	273	298	302	319	328	318	195	151	144	204	248	271
Construction	727	869	977	934	1,007	1,174	1,809	2,720	4,949	7,719	15,854	25,546	31,959	34,764	42,791
Tradeᶜ	722	807	958	1,008	1,068	1,177	1,554	2,355	3,045	3,897	6,180	8,507	11,049	13,912	17,541
Transportation, storage, communications	938	1,010	1,173	1,243	1,479	1,567	2,121	2,718	3,946	2,310	4,077	6,775	9,960	12,764	15,012
Finance, insurance, business services															
Ownership of dwellings	494	545	601	661	727	800	1,000	1,333	2,000	3,425	5,278	6,924	7,632	9,663	10,962
Othersᵈ	232	276	292	309	327	361	472	682	1,030	1,688	2,619	3,278	3,511	4,175	4,574
Other private services	171	191	215	238	265	297	339	403	523	1,281	1,989	2,609	3,293	4,155	5,261
Government services	1,366	1,449	1,615	1,678	1,805	2,145	2,533	3,490	4,990	4,990	7,890	9,720	15,146	18,912	23,384
Gross domestic product	12,931	14,431	15,704	17,153	22,581	27,858	40,088	98,839	133,834	139,223	163,892	203,942	223,818	247,622	384,236

SOURCES: SAMA, *Annual Report 1979*, p. 112–13; ibid., *1975*, pp. 130–31; ibid., *1976*, pp. 144–45; ibid., *1977*, pp. 146–47; ibid., *1978*, pp. 166–67; ibid., *1979*, pp. 165–66; ibid., *1981*, pp. 1969–70

ᵃ Based on revised system of prices.
ᵇ Preliminary estimates.
ᶜ Includes wholesale and retail trade, restaurants and hotels.
ᵈ Less imputed bank service charges.

TABLE A-4

Gross Domestic Product by Economic Activity
(At constant 1970 factor prices: million Saudi riyals)

Sector	1967	1968	1969	1970	1971	1972	1973	1974	1975	1975[a]	1976[a]	1977[a]	1978[a]	1979[a]	1980[a,b]
Agriculture, forestry, fishing	885	925	957	984	1,018	1,050	1,089	1,130	1,174	1,174	1,221	1,282	1,483	1,550	1,639
Mining, quarrying															
Crude petroleum, natural gas	6,177	6,696	7,085	8,106	9,922	12,427	15,556	18,158	17,339	17,339	17,510	19,852	19,650	20,112	21,652
Others	40	46	51	47	49	55	77	96	121	81	112	134	147	125	128
Manufacturing															
Petroleum refining	780	920	1,016	1,241	1,355	1,304	1,378	1,417	1,300	1,300	1,359	1,523	1,591	1,689	1,795
Others	309	344	385	431	484	543	599	665	740	721	828	956	1,103	1,276	1,477
Electricity, gas, water	198	219	247	273	298	329	381	417	459	322	345	414	546	725	868
Construction	847	961	1,028	934	957	1,053	1,396	1,737	2,189	2,461	3,309	4,146	4,582	4,700	5,091
Trade[c]	755	841	961	1,008	1,051	1,146	1,375	1,623	1,934	1,920	2,331	2,881	3,555	4,272	5,130
Transportation, storage, communications	919	1,013	1,140	1,243	1,468	1,544	1,849	2,224	2,721	1,289	1,580	1,929	2,367	2,729	3,031
Finance, insurance, business services															
Ownership of dwellings	521	565	602	661	693	732	787	864	951	1,650	1,933	2,276	2,549	2,804	3,084
Others[d]	251	291	297	309	312	332	378	428	484	526	605	700	769	875	972
Other private services	180	198	215	238	253	272	287	311	336	319	363	413	470	534	611
Government services	1,475	1,516	1,647	1,678	1,722	1,834	1,981	2,177	2,438	2,438	2,755	2,813	2,953	3,130	3,333
Gross domestic product	13,336	14,535	15,628	17,153	19,582	22,621	27,133	31,246	32,186	31,539	34,250	39,318	41,765	44,521	48,811

SOURCES: SAMA, *Annual Report 1975*, pp. 114–15; ibid., *1975*, pp. 132–33; ibid., *1976*, pp. 146–47; ibid., *1977*, pp. 148–49; ibid., *1978*, pp. 168–69; ibid., *1979*, pp. 167–68; ibid., *1981*, pp. 171–72.

[a] Based on revised system of prices.
[b] Preliminary estimates.
[c] Includes wholesale and retail trade, restaurants and hotels.
[d] Less imputed bank service charges.

TABLE A-5

Expenditure on Gross Domestic Product
(At current market prices: million Saudi riyals)

Expenditure Category	1968	1969	1970	1971	1972	1973	1974	1975	1975[a]	1976[a]	1977[a]	1978[a]	1979[a]	1980[a,b]
Government consumption	2,747	3,026	3,421	3,789	4,285	5,335	9,864	15,911	15,911	28,883	41,033	47,034	71,904	88,206
Private consumption	4,585	5,360	5,859	6,412	6,915	7,895	9,827	13,828	18,039	23,903	34,372	54,607	60,845	70,186
Gross fixed capital formation	2,392	2,632	2,597	2,931	3,403	5,694	8,400	14,866	17,699	33,540	51,191	66,891	76,654	94,977
By sector														
Government	1,123	1,349	1,214	1,204	1,443	1,985	3,416	7,348	7,370	17,491	27,352	40,484	49,031	61,598
Non-oil private sector	884	941	1,056	1,150	1,290	1,669	2,351	3,859	6,670	10,627	16,523	18,354	19,401	23,183
Oil sector	385	342	327	577	670	2,040	2,633	3,659	3,659	5,422	7,316	8,053	8,222	10,196
By type														
Construction		2,067	1,969	2,195	2,595	4,706	6,214	11,505	13,222	26,888	37,684	51,542	63,412	76,864
Transport equipment		270	309	313	335	468	757	1,331	2,253	3,539	5,491	6,391	6,756	6,911
Machinery		295	319	423	473	520	1,429	2,030	2,021	2,798	7,546	7,778	5,926	10,685
Other capital goods									203	315	470	1,180	560	517
Increase in stocks[c]	735	722	209	-205	95	-113	835	2,402	748	780	838	7,611	379	4,869
Exports of goods and services	8,589	9,086	10,302	15,189	19,862	30,012	85,682	114,461	114,461	120,284	140,321	140,762	147,236	262,566
Less: Import of goods and services	4,392	4,851	4,990	5,205	6,302	8,272	15,293	27,257	27,257	42,863	62,699	91,505	107,479	134,351
Expenditure on GDP	14,657	15,975	17,399	22,920	28,258	40,551	99,315	134,211	139,600	164,526	205,056	225,400	249,539	386,453

SOURCES: SAMA *Annual Report 1975*, p. 134; ibid., *1976*, p. 148; ibid., *1977*, p. 150; ibid., *1978*, p. 169; ibid., *1981*, p. 173; *Statistical Summary 1979*, p. 78; ibid., *1980*, p. 90.

[a] Revised estimates. [b] Preliminary estimates. [c] Includes errors and omissions.

TABLE A-6

Employment by Economic Activity
(*In thousands*)

Sector	1967[a]	1970[b]	1975	1980
Agriculture	714.2	727.1	695.0	598.8
Mining	1.5	1.8	3.4	7.3
Oil and refineries	15.8	17.2	27.4	36.0
Manufacturing	48.9	58.2	74.4	104.2
Utilities	8.0	10.7	16.1	31.5
Construction	61.6	77.6	172.3	330.1
Trade	81.3	91.6	153.6	310.6
Transportation	53.2	68.9	114.5	214.6
Finance and business services	– [c]	10.8	13.1	34.8
Other private services	145.0	167.9	230.0	482.3
Public services[d]	139.1	164.7	246.7	321.0
Total	1268.6	1396.5	1746.5	2471.2

SOURCES: K.O.S.A., *First Development Plan*, pp. 75, 81; ibid., *Second Development Plan*, pp. 11, 63; ibid., *Third Development Plan*, p. 37.

[a] Estimated using average annual sectoral growth rates for 1966–70 obtained from the First Development Plan.

[b] Estimated using average annual sectoral growth rates for 1970–75 obtained from the Second Development Plan.

[c] Included in employment data for trade.

[d] Civilian employment only.

TABLE A-7

Size of Armed Forces

Military Branch	1965	1976	1980
Army	18,000	40,000	34,500
Navy	n.a.	1,500	1,500
Air Force	n.a.	5,500	17,000
Frontier Force and Coast Guard	n.a.	6,500	10,000
National Guard	18,000	16,000	20,000
Total	40,000	69,500	82,500

SOURCES: Walpole, *Area Handbook for Saudi Arabia*, p. 326; Nyrop, *Area Handbook for Saudi Arabia*, pp. 321–22; Shaw and Long, *Saudi Arabian Modernization*, pp. 67–72.

n.a.–not available.

TABLE A-8

Gross Domestic Income, 1970 and 1980
(*At 1970 factor prices: million Saudi riyals*)

	1970	1980 Excluding Terms of Trade Effect	Including Terms of Trade Effect
Petroleum	9,347	23,447[a]	114,790[b]
Other sectors	7,655	25,364	25,364
Total	17,002	48,811	140,154

SOURCES: Tables A-3, A-4; World Bank, *World Tables 1980*, pp 226–27; United Nations Conference on Trade and Development, *Handbook of International Trade and Development Statistics*, 1981 Supplement, p. 451.

NOTE: Based on revised system of prices.

[a] Value added in the petroleum sector deflated by the index of petroleum prices.

[b] Value added in the petroleum sector deflated by the import price index. This index was calculated by using the implicit deflator of imports of goods and nonfactor services for 1970–77, and the unit value index for imports for 1977–80.

TABLE A-9

Sources of Growth of the Non-oil Economy, 1967–80

	1967	1980
Productivity (SR thousand per worker)[a,b]	4,183	8,848
Labor force (thousand)[c]	1,293	2,518
Labor force, without additional labor imports during 1967–80 (thousand)[c]	1,293	1,709
Non-oil GDP (SR million)[a,b]		
Actual	5,408	22,280
With constant labor force during 1967–80	5,408	11,441
Without additional labor imports during 1967–80	5,408	15,122

SOURCES: Tables A-4, A-6, A-7; Birks and Sinclair, *Arab Manpower*, p. 107; Chamieh, *Saudi Arabia Yearbook*, p. 266; Walpole, *Area Handbook*, p. 260.

[a] At constant 1970 prices, based on the revised system of prices.
[b] Does not include ownership of dwellings.
[c] Includes civilian and military manpower.

TABLE A-10

Incremental Capital Output Ratio
1965-73 and 1973-77

t_o	t_n	$Y_{t_n} - Y_{t_o}$	$\sum_{t_o}^{t_n - 1} I_t$	ICOR
1965	1973	16,379	21,593	1.32
1973	1977	13,635	54,183	3.97

Y_t = Gross domestic product (SR millions) at constant 1970 prices, in period t

I_t = Gross domestic investments (SR millions) at constant 1970 prices, in period t

$$\text{ICOR} = \frac{Y_{t_n} - Y_{t_o}}{\sum_{t_o}^{t_n - 1} I_t}$$

SOURCE: World Bank, *World Tables, 1980*, pp. 226-27.

APPENDIX B

The House of al-Sa'ud

King 'Abd al-'Aziz Ibn Sa'ud
b. 1880
r. 1902–53

Living brothers
Ahmad
'Abd al-Rahman
Mu'said

Fourteen wives, including:

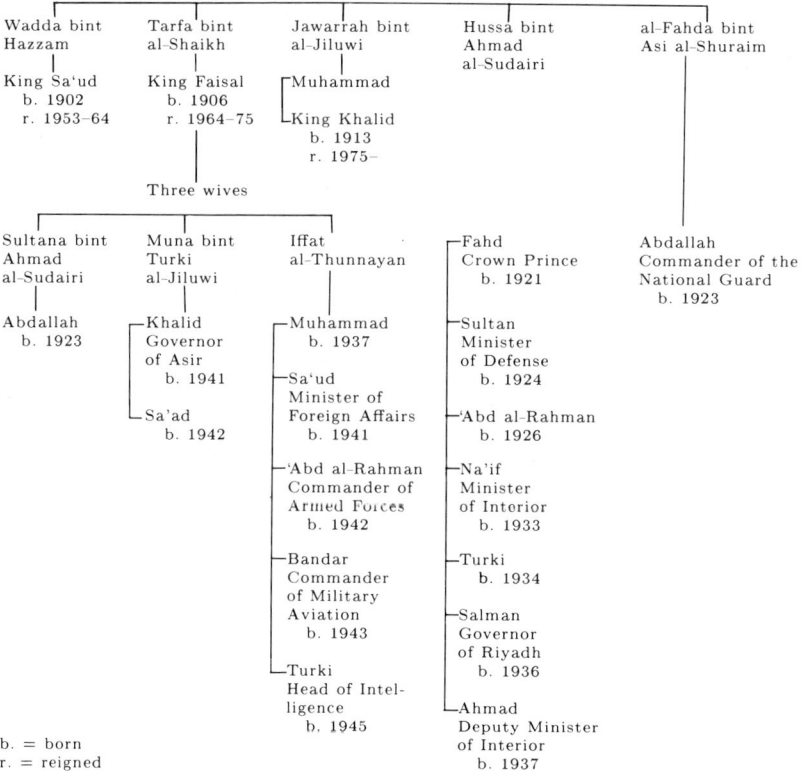

Wadda bint Hazzam	Tarfa bint al-Shaikh	Jawarrah bint al-Jiluwi	Hussa bint Ahmad al-Sudairi	al-Fahda bint Asi al-Shuraim
King Sa'ud b. 1902 r. 1953–64	King Faisal b. 1906 r. 1964–75	Muhammad / King Khalid b. 1913 r. 1975–		

Three wives

Sultana bint Ahmad al-Sudairi	Muna bint Turki al-Jiluwi	Iffat al-Thunnayan		Abdallah Commander of the National Guard b. 1923
Abdallah b. 1923	Khalid Governor of Asir b. 1941	Muhammad b. 1937	Fahd Crown Prince b. 1921	
	Sa'ad b. 1942	Sa'ud Minister of Foreign Affairs b. 1941	Sultan Minister of Defense b. 1924	
		'Abd al-Rahman Commander of Armed Forces b. 1942	'Abd al-Rahman b. 1926	
		Bandar Commander of Military Aviation b. 1943	Na'if Minister of Interior b. 1933	
		Turki Head of Intelligence b. 1945	Turki b. 1934	
			Salman Governor of Riyadh b. 1936	
			Ahmad Deputy Minister of Interior b. 1937	

b. = born
r. = reigned

SOURCE: House Committee on Foreign Affairs, *Saudi Arabia and the United States*, p. 18.

Notes

CHAPTER ONE

1. The concept of segmented society, as used here was developed by E. E. Evans-Pritchard in his study of the Sanusi and his earlier writings on the Nuer. See his *The Sansui of Cyrenaica* (Oxford: Oxford University Press, 1949 and *The Nuer* (Oxford: Oxford University Press, 1940).

2. For a study of traditional Arabia, see H. St. John Philby, *Empty Quarter* (London: Constable, 1933); Charles Doughty, *Travels in Arabia Deserta* (New York: Liverright, 1926); William Palgrave, *Narrative of a Year's Journey Through Central and Eastern Arabia, 1862–1863* (London: Macmillan and Co., 1866); and a most important source, John Lewis Burckhardt, *Notes on the Bedouins and Wahabys* (London: H. Colburn and R. Bentley, 1830).

3. For the history of this period see the works by H. St. John Philby, who was a British agent sent to the Saudis to encourage and advise them in their conflict with the Ottomans. See in particular his autobiography, *Arabian Days* (London: Robert Hale, 1948) and his account of the Saudi royal family in *Arabian Jubilee* (London: Robert Hale, 1952). For a critical look at this development see "Da'a'im al-Nizam al-Saudi," *Saut al-Tali'ah* 1 (April 1973): 5–17. A radical opponent of the Saudis, Nasir al-Sa'id, now imprisoned in Saudi Arabia, has done an extensive and not always responsible study of Saudi history. See his *Tarikh Al-i Sa'ud* (Beirut, 1979). For the importance of the role of religion in the formation of the state see

Christine Helms, *The Cohesion of Saudi Arabia: Evolution of Political Identity* (London: Croom Helm, 1981).

4. Helen Lackner, *A House Built on Sand: A Political Economy of Saudi Arabia* (London: Ithaca Press, 1978), pp. 16–21.

5. Exclusivism is one of the conditions that David Apter considers important to the functioning of a modernizing autocracy. See his "System Process, and Politics of Economic Development," in *Industrialization and Society,* ed. B. F. Hoselitz and W. E. Moore (The Hague: Mouton, 1963), pp. 139–40.

6. Labid [pseud.], "Al-Ikhwan," *Saut al-Tali'ah* 1 (June 1973): 8–39.

7. Following the defeat, the Ikhwan settlements were either destroyed or abandoned. See Lackner, *A House Built on Sand,* p. 27.

8. The important leaders of the settlements were men like Sultan Ibn Bijad, the sheik of the Ghat Ghat tribe; Dhaidhan Ibn Hithlin, the Ajman sheik; and Saud Ibn Lami, the head of the Matiri tribe. See Labid, "Al-Ikhwan," pp. 36–39.

9. Joseph Kraft, "Letter from Saudi Arabia," *The New Yorker,* 20 October 1975, p. 126.

10. Adham was influential enough to have his nephew Turki, the late Faisal's son, succeed him in his position as head of intelligence.

CHAPTER TWO

1. William Rugh, "The Emergence of a New Middle Class in Saudi Arabia," *Middle East Journal* 27 (Winter 1973): 12–13.

2. Adeed I. Dawisha, "Internal Values and External Threats: The Making of Saudi Foreign Policy," *Orbis* (Spring 1979): 132.

3. Richard F. Nyrop et al., *Area Handbook for Saudi Arabia,* 3d ed. (Washington, D.C.: GPO, 1977), pp. 182–83.

4. Dawisha, "Internal Values and External Threats," p. 132.

5. Ibrahim al-Awaji, *Bureaucracy and Society in Saudi Arabia* (Ph.D. diss., University of Virginia, 1971), p. 123.

6. Talal Asad Murshid, *Saudi Arabia: Administrative Aspects of Development* (Ph.D. diss., Claremont University, 1978), p. 174–75.

7. Othman Yasin al-Rawaf, *The Concept of Five Crises in Political Development—Relevance to the Kingdom of Saudi Arabia* (Ph.D. diss., Duke University, 1980), p. 483.

8. Nyrop, *Area Handbook,* p. 177.

9. Hani Yousef Khashoggi, *Local Administration in Saudi Arabia* (Ph.D. diss., Claremont University, 1979), pp. 121–23; al-Awaji, *Bureaucracy and Society,* p. 131. For a study of the regional characteristics and the actual form of local governments, see Ahmid Rashid, *Al-Idarah al-Mahalliyah fi al-Mamlikah al-'Arabiyah al-Sa'udiyah* (Cairo: Dar al-Sharq, 1981).

10. Soliman A. Solaim, *Constitutional and Judicial Organization in Saudi Arabia* (Ph.D. diss., Johns Hopkins University, 1970), p. 406. See Rashid, *Al-Mamlikah al-'Arabiyah al-Sa'udiyah* and Wizarah al-'Adl, *Nizam al-Qadha* (Riyadh: Matabi al-Hukumah, 1975) for the new legal order that placed the judiciary under the authority of the government.

11. The list includes many educated and able officials such as Yusuf al-Hamadan, former deputy minister of commerce; 'Abd al-'Aziz Dukhyal, former deputy minister of finance; and Ahmad Sirraj, assistant secretary of foreign affairs. For further information regarding the changes among the senior officials, see John A. Shaw and David E. Long, *Saudi Arabian Modernization* (New York: Praeger, 1982), pp. 75–76.

12. Cited in al-Rawaf, *The Concept of Five Crises,* p. 491.

13. For information on the structural format of the Saudi political system, see the organizational diagrams in Fouad al-Farsy, *Saudi Arabia: A Case Study in Development* (London: Stacey International, 1978), pp. 70–74, 96–125; and Nyrop, *Area Handbook,* pp. 178–82.

14. "Saudis Will Pay for Repairs on Iraq's Reactor," *New York Times,* 17 July 1981.

15. Editorial, "Districts System Reform," *Saudi Business and Arab Economic Report,* 13 July 1981, pp. 18–20.

16. Cited in al-Rawaf, *The Concept of Five Crises,* p. 478.

17. Khashoggi, *Local Administration in Saudi Arabia,* p. 127.

18. Kingdom of Saudi Arabia (K.O.S.A.), Ministry of Planning, *The Second Development Plan 1395–1400 (1975–1980)* (Riyadh: Ministry of Planning, 1975), pp. 422–25.

19. Stockholm International Peace Research Institute, *World Armaments and Disarmament, SIPRI Yearbook 1978* (Cambridge, Mass.: MIT Press, 1978), pp. 148–49.

20. Ibid., p. 137.

21. U.S. Congress, House Committee on Foreign Affairs, *United States Arms Policies in the Persian Gulf and Red Sea Areas,* 95th Cong., 1st sess. (Washington, D.C.: GPO, 1977), p. 247.

22. Kraft, "Letter from Saudi Arabia," p. 127.

23. House Committee on Foreign Affairs, *United States Arms Policies*, p. 28.

24. U.S. Congress, House Committee on Foreign Affairs, Subcommittee on Europe and the Middle East, *Saudi Arabia and the United States: The New Context in an Evolving "Special Relationship."* Report prepared by the Foreign Affairs and National Defense Division, Congressional Research Service, Library of Congress, 97th Cong., 1st sess. (Washington, D.C.: GPO, 1981), pp. 46–47; and ibid., p. 21.

25. U.S. Congress, Senate Committee on Foreign Relations, *The Sale of F-15s to Saudi Arabia.* Report prepared by Hans Binnendijk and Bill Richardson, 95th Cong., 2d sess. (Washington, D.C.: GPO, 1978), p. 247.

26. Fred Halliday, "A Curious and Close Liaison: Saudi Arabia's Relations with the United States," in *State, Society and Economy in Saudi Arabia,* ed. Tim Niblock (London: Croom Helm, 1982), p. 140.

27. House Committee on Foreign Affairs, *United States Arms Policies*, pp. 35–36; House Subcommittee on Europe and the Middle East, *Saudi Arabia and the United States*, pp. 46–57.

28. Senate Committee on Foreign Relations, *Sale of F-15s to Saudi Arabia*, p. 247.

29. House Committee on Foreign Affairs, *United States Arms Policies*, p. 21.

30. Ibid., p. 31.

31. For an enlightening look at the history of the military structure and its inherent weaknesses see "Al-Quwat al-Mussallaha," *Saut al-Tali'ah* 2 (January 1974): 8–34.

32. For the extent of OPGDE's jurisdiction to arrest and judge those accused of having broken the Quranic injunctions or the tradition of the Prophet and the last four caliphs, see the bill defining the jurisdiction of OPGDE and an interview with 'Abd al-'Aziz ibn Ibrahim Al al-Shaikh, the director of OPGDE, *Al-Riyadh*, 4 March 1981.

33. Fighting in the Great Mosque is among the most reprehensible acts a Muslim can commit. Yet thirty of the ulema were willing to issue a *fatwa* (legal opinion with religious sanction) authorizing the troops to use arms in the mosque should the rebels refuse to surrender, see *Al-Riyadh*, 11 November 1979. The *fatwa* that authorized Saud's abdication had eleven signatories, see Hafiz Wahba, *Arabian Days* (London: Arthur Baker, 1965), p. 179.

34. Pranaye B. Gupte, "Saudi Arabia's Path to Prosperity," *New York Times*, 26 March 1981.

35. Rugh, "Emergence of a New Middle Class," p. 20.

36. "Ha'iat al-Amr bi al-Ma'ruf wa al-Nahi 'An al-Munkar," *Saut al-Tali'ah* 2 (April 1974): 10–30.

37. Of particular interest in this area is a class analysis of Arabia published by the Socialist party of Arabia (Hizb al-'Amal al-Ishtirakiyah al-'Arabiyah, *Al-Wadh al-Tabaqi fi al-Jazirah al-'Arabiyah* (n.p.).

CHAPTER THREE

1. See table A-1, Appendix A.

2. World Bank, *World Development Report 1982* (New York: Oxford University Press, 1982), p. 111.

3. See table A-8, Appendix A.

4. Estimated from data in tables 4 and A-6, Appendix A.

5. The following equation was used to separate the effects of the increase in national and nonnational labor force as well as higher productivity on expansion of output:

$$Y_{1980} - Y_{1970} = L_{1970} \left(y_{1980} - y_{1970} \right) + y_{1980} \left(L^*_{1980} - L_{1970} \right) + y_{1980} \left(L_{1980} - L^*_{1980} \right)$$

where:

Y = non-oil GDP

L = actual labor force

L^*_{1980} = employment in 1980 with no influx of additional labor during 1970–80

y = labor productivity = Y/L

$L_{1970} \left(y_{1980} - y_{1970} \right)$ = change in output due to higher productivity

$y_{1980} \left(L^*_{1980} - L_{1970} \right)$ = change in output due to increase in national labor force

$y_{1980} \left(L_{1980} - L^*_{1980} \right)$ = change in output due to increase in nonnational labor force

6. World Bank, *World Tables 1980* (Baltimore: Johns Hopkins University Press, 1980), p. 227.

7. . In 1980, imports of agricultural and industrial goods were SR 15.8 billion and SR 84.6 billion respectively. Gross value added

in agriculture was SR 4.6 billion and that of industry (other than petroleum refining) was SR 8.1 billion. See table A-2, Appendix A; and United Nations, *Yearbook of International Trade Statistics 1980,* vol. 1 (New York: U.N., 1981), pp. 833–35.

8. J. S. Birks and C. A. Sinclair, *Arab Manpower, The Crisis of Development* (London: Croom Helm, 1980), p. 108.

9. The low value added per worker in this sector cannot be attributed to the low wages of domestic servants. In early 1977, the average salary of a servant was SR 18,000 per year. See Ragaei El Mallakh, *Saudi Arabia, Rush to Development* (London: Croom Helm, 1982), p. 421.

10. Estimated using the wage rate of production workers in 1978 and the increase in average wage income in the construction sector between 1978 and 1980. See K.O.S.A., Ministry of Finance and National Economy, Central Department of Statistics, *Statistical Indicators 1400 (1980)* (Riyadh: Central Department of Statistics, 1980), p. 49; K.O.S.A., Ministry of Finance and National Economy, Central Department of Statistics, *Statistical Yearbook 1400 (1980)* (Riyadh: Central Department of Statistics, 1980), p. 501.

11. K.O.S.A., *Statistical Indicators 1980,* p. 49; K.O.S.A., *Statistical Yearbook 1980,* p. 501.

CHAPTER FOUR

1. Calculated from data in tables A-3, A-6, A-7, Appendix A.

2. World Bank, *World Development Report 1980,* p. 149.

3. Ibid., pp. 111, 149; and United Nations, Economic Commission for Western Asia, *The Population Situation in the ECWA Region, Saudi Arabia* (Beirut: U.N., Economic Commission for Western Asia, 1979), pp. 11.4, 11.5.

4. In Iran the share of the three largest cities was 37 percent in 1976. See World Bank, *World Development Report 1980,* pp. 111, 149; and United Nations, *Demographic Yearbook 1978* (New York: U.N., 1979), p. 220.

5. In 1976 Tehran's population was 4.5 million while Isfahan's was 672,000. See World Bank, *World Development Report 1980,* pp. 111, 149; and U.N., *Demographic Yearbook 1978,* p. 220.

6. In 1974, the population of Riyadh was 667,000 and that of Mecca 367,000. See U.N., *The Population Situation,* p. 11.5.

7. K.O.S.A., *Statistical Indicators 1980,* pp. 169–74.

8. Especially in those countries where the supply of educated manpower is large enough to enable them to export a sizable number.

9. Ralph Braibanti, and Fouad Abdul-Salam Al-Farsy, "Saudi Arabia: A Developmental Perspective," *Journal of South Asian and Middle Eastern Studies* 1 (Fall 1977): 16–17. Al-Farsy was assistant deputy minister.

10. Fiches du Monde Arabe, *Arab World File,* "Saudi Arabia" (Nicosia, Cyprus: Fiches du Monde Arabe), 28 January 1981, 1-Sa28a.

11. U.N., *The Population Situation*, pp. 11.5, 11.16; and K.O.S.A., *Statistical Indicators 1980,* p. 176.

12. K.O.S.A., *Statistical Yearbook 1980,* p. 107.

13. Ibid., pp. 87–95, 108–11.

14. Walpole, *Area Handbook,* pp. 258–59.

15. These are positions that require at least the completion of primary education.

16. K.O.S.A., Central Planning Organization, *The First Development Plan 1390–1395 (1970–1975)* (Riyadh: Central Planning Organization, 1970), p. 78.

17. Rugh, "The Emergence of a New Middle Class," p. 9.

18. K.O.S.A., *Statistical Yearbook 1980,* p. 501.

19. According to one estimate, in 1980, there were about 1,200,000 expatriate workers in Saudi Arabia: 600,000 from North Yemen, 250,000 from Egypt, 200,000 from Pakistan, 80,000 from South Korea, 70,000 from the Philippines, and 25,000 to 30,000 from the United Kingdom and the United States. See the Economist Intelligence Unit, *Quarterly Economic Review of Saudi Arabia* (Annual Supplement, 1982), p. 6.

20. International Monetary Fund (IMF), *Balance of Payments Yearbook 1980* (Washington, D.C.: IMF, 1980), p. 472; and IMF, *Balance of Payments Statistics 1982* (Washington, D.C.: IMF, 1982), p. 456.

21. K.O.S.A., *Statistical Yearbook 1979,* p. 192.

22. Calculated from data in United Nations, Educational, Scientific and Cultural Organization (UNESCO), *Statistical Yearbook 1980* (Paris: UNESCO, 1980), pp. 1126–27; and IMF, *International Financial Statistics 1982* (Washington, D.C.: IMF, 1982), pp. 248–49, 390–91.

23. Calculated from data in Motoko Katakura, *Bedouin Village, A Study of a Saudi Arabian People in Transition* (Tokyo: Tokyo University Press, 1977), p. 116.

24. World Bank, *World Tables 1980*, p. 226.

25. Calculated from data in Katakura, *Bedouin Village*, pp. 111, 116.

26. U.N., *Statistical Yearbook 1978*, p. 952.

27. Calculated from data in K.O.S.A., *Statistical Yearbook 1979*, pp. 236, 238; and Jebran Chamieh, ed., *Saudi Arabia Yearbook 1980–81* (Sin el Fin, Lebanon: The Research and Publishing House, 1980), p. 266.

28. This phenomenon occurs when the consumption of one group causes a rise in the material aspirations of other groups.

29. Those with populations greater than one million.

30. From a lecture given at the Tayef Literary Club, June 1977, excerpts printed in Chamieh, *Saudi Arabia Yearbook*, p. 145.

CHAPTER FIVE

1. Calculated from data in Ramon Knauerhase, *The Saudi Arabian Economy*, (New York: Praeger, 1975), p. 282; World Bank, *World Tables 1980*, p. 226; Paul Barker, *Saudi Arabia: The Development Dilemma* (London: Economist Intellligence Unit, 1982), p. 10; and K.O.S.A., Saudi Arabian Monetary Agency (SAMA), *Annual Report 1401 (1981)* (Riyadh: SAMA, 1981), p, 170.

2. World Bank, *World Development Report 1982*, p. 119.

3. International Institute for Strategic Studies, *The Military Balance, 1981–1982* (London: International Institute for Strategic Studies, 1981), pp. 112–13.

4. Estimated from data in K.O.S.A., *Statistical Indicators 1980*, p. 49; and K.O.S.A., *Statistical Yearbook 1980*, p. 501.

5. Estimated from data in International Institute for Strategic Studies, *The Military Balance, 1981–1982*, p. 113; and tables 17 and A-7, Appendix A.

6. ICOR is the dollars of investment required to expand domestic product by one dollar.

7. To highlight the enormous size of this investment, it suffices to mention that the total aid required by Lebanon for the reconstruction of its war-torn economy will be about $15 billion over the next ten years. See the Economist Intelligence Unit, *Quarterly Economic Review of Saudi Arabia* (Second Quarter 1981), p. 15; and "Western Nations Consider Aid for War-torn Lebanon," *Wall Street Journal*, 21 July 1983, p. 28.

8. Hayyan Ibn-Bayyan [pseud.], "Poor Little Rich Nation, Open Letter to Saudi Arabia," *Nation,* 4 April 1981, p. 401.

9. Edmond O'Sullivan, "High Finance Favors the Big Firms," *Middle East Economic Digest,* 20 March 1981, p. 39.

10. The word *bedouin* is derived from *badw,* which refers to a desert inhabitant. See Katakura, *Bedouin Village,* p. 177, and Jere L. Bacharach, *A Near East Studies Handbook,* rev. ed. (Seattle and London: University of Washington Press, 1976), p. 99. The word *sheik* means "head of a tribe; leader of a village." See Bacharach, *Handbook,* p. 109.

11. John Whelan, "Saudi Arabia: Small Business Chafes under Barons' Hold on Big Contracts," *Middle East Economic Digest,* 17 March 1978, p. 3.

12. Lackner, *A House Built on Sand,* p. 208.

13. Nancy A. Shilling, *Doing Business in Saudi Arabia and the Arab Gulf States* (New York: Inter-Cresent Publishing and Information Corporation, 1979), p. 365.

14. Medium-sized firms are those employing fewer than fifty, but more than nine workers.

15. K.O.S.A., *Third Development Plan,* pp. 68, 354–55.

16. K.O.S.A., *Statistical Yearbook 1980,* p. 210.

17. K.O.S.A., *Third Development Plan,* pp. 155–56, 275.

18. J. S. Birks and C. A. Sinclair, "The Domestic Political Economy of Development in Saudi Arabia," in Tim Niblock, ed., *State, Society and Economy in Saudi Arabia* (London: Croom Helm, 1982), p. 204.

19. K.O.S.A., *Third Development Plan,* p. 276.

20. Ibid., pp. 275, 442.

21. Ibid., pp. 54–55.

22. Since value added in public services is mainly made up of wages and salaries, we use the price deflator for this sector as an index of wages and salaries in the public sector.

23. To cover administrative costs, a service charge of 2 to 3 percent per annum is charged on the outstanding balance of loans.

24. K.O.S.A., *Third Development Plan,* pp. 249–50.

25. Ibid., p. 274.

26. Ibid., p. 250.

27. Fouad A. Al-Farsy, "Saudi Arabian Industrial Development: Aspirations and Realities," in Ragaei El Mallakh and Dorothea H. El Mallakh, eds., *Saudi Arabia: Energy Developmental Planning, and Industrialization* (Lexington, Mass.: Lexington Books, 1982), p. 24.

28. El Mallakh, *Saudi Arabia, Rush to Development,* p. 431.

29. Calculated from data in K.O.S.A., *Third Development Plan,* p. 251.

30. Computed from data in ibid., p. 274.

31. Al-Farsy, "Saudi Arabian Industrial Development," p. 24; and Robert E. Looney, *Saudi Arabia's Development Potential* (Lexington, Mass.: Lexington Books, 1982), pp. 172–73.

32. K.O.S.A., *Third Development Plan,* p. 231; and K.O.S.A., *Statistical Indicators 1980,* p. 38.

CHAPTER SIX

1. Philip Taubman, "U.S. Aides Say Corruption Is Threat to Saudi Stability," *New York Times,* 16 April 1980. Note in this article the comment by Frank Jungers, former chairman of Aramco that "the corruption has been accepted and unquestioned."

2. On congruence between the state and society, see Robert Lacey, *The Kingdom* (New York: Harcourt Brace Jovanovich, 1982), pp. 504–13.

3. State Department, Division of Research for Near East, South Asia, and Africa, *Saudi Arabia: A Disruptive Force in Western Arabia,* Intelligence Report, no. 7144, 16 January 1956, p. 5.

4. Ibid.

5. U.S. Congress, Senate Committee on Foreign Relations, Subcommittee on Multinationals, *Overview of U.S./Saudi Arabia Relations and Areas of Conflict, Description of and U.S. Involvement in Accelerating Saudi Arabia's Domestic and Military Modernization Programs,* 94th Cong., 1st sess., 29 July 1975, p. 434.

6. Senate Committee on Foreign Relations, Subcommittee on Multinationals, Hearings, 94th Cong., 1st sess., 9–10 June 1975, p. 180.

7. Senate Committee on Foreign Relations, Subcommittee on Multinationals, Hearings, 94th Cong., 2d sess., 4 May 1976, p. 435.

8. Senate Committee on Foreign Relations, Subcommittee on Multinationals, Hearing, 94th Cong., 1st sess., 13, 20 May and 10, 13 June 1975, p. 139; 94th Cong., 1st sess., 11 September 1975, p. 139; and 95th Cong., 1st sess., 7 April 1976, p. 435.

9. U.S. Congress, House Committee on Foreign Affairs, Hearings, 94th Cong., 1st sess., 29 July 1975, p. 198.

10. Edward R. F. Sheehan, "The Epidemic of Money," *New York Times Magazine,* 14 November 1976, p. 118.

11. David Ignatius, "Royal Payoffs: Some Saudi Princes Pressure Oil Firms for Secret Payments," *Wall Street Journal*, 1 May 1981.

12. David Ignatius, "Royal Payoffs: Big Saudi Oil Deal with Italy Collapses after Fee Plan Is Barred," *Wall Street Journal*, 4 May 1981.

13. Taubman, "U.S. Aides Say Corruption Is Threat."

14. Sheehan, "The Epidemic of Money," p. 118.

15. Amnesty International has no report of political prisoners or torture in Saudi jails. Prisoners are often released early, see Lacey, *The Kingdom*, pp. 504–7. For a contradictory but not convincing interpretation, see *Human Rights in the Arabian Peninsula "Saudi Arabia"* (Saut al-Tali'ah, n.d.).

16. State Department, *Saudi Arabia: A Disruptive Force*, pp. ii, iii.

17. State Department, *Saudi Arabia: A Disruptive Force*, p. 7.

18. Lackner, *A House Built on Sand*, p. 102; House Committee on Foreign Affairs, *U.S. Arms Policies*, p. 20.

19. Lackner, *A House Built on Sand*, p. 102.

20. The four princes who escaped to Egypt included Talal, Badr, Fawaz (all brothers of the king), and Sa'd ibn Fahd (a cousin). For an account of family rivalry in this period see Lacey, *The Kingdom*, pp. 321–42.

21. Michael Collins, "Jobs, Jobs, Jobs."

22. Fred Halliday, *Arabia without Sultans: A Political Survey of Instability in the Arab World* (New York: Vintage Books, 1975), pp. 80–81; Lackner, *A House Built on Sand*, p. 96.

23. Lackner, *A House Built on Sand*, p. 97.

24. Salah [pseud.], "Al -Mu'aridah al-Siyasiyah fi al-Sa'udiyah," *Saut al-Tali'ah* 1 (March 1973): 18–29; and *Struggle, Oppression and Counter Revolution*, a pamphlet cited by Lackner in *A House Built on Sand*, p. 98.

25. Lackner, *A House Built on Sand*, p. 104; Halliday, *Arabia without Sultans*, p. 81.

26. *Political Opposition in Saudi Arabia* (San Francisco: Saut al-Tali'ah, 1980), pp. 15–16.

27. Lackner, *A House Built on Sand*, p. 104; Halliday, *Arabia without Sultans*, p. 80.

28. Cited in David Holden and Richard Johns, *The House of Saud* (London: Pan Books, 1981), p. 515.

29. Michael Collins, "Jobs, Jobs, Jobs ... and Too Few Saudis to Fill Them," *Christian Science Monitor,* 26 January 1983.

30. Holden and Johns, *The House of Saud,* pp. 518–19.

31. For the accounts of the mosque take-over, see John Nielsen et al., "Saudi Arabia: A Shaky U.S. Pillar of Security," *Newsweek,* 3 March 1980, pp. 34–38; "Sacrilege in Mecca," *Time,* 3 December 1979, pp. 50–51; and Steven Strasser et al., "The Khomeini Contagion," *Newsweek,* 17 December 1979, pp. 39–40.

32. "Al-Qatif," *Saut al-Tali'ah* 22 (May 1980): 190–91; Arnold Hottinger, "Who Held the Grand Mosque Hostage?" *New York Review of Books,* 6 March 1980, p. 35; Arnold Hottinger, "The Rich Arab States in Trouble," *New York Review of Books,* 15 May 1980, pp. 23–24. See also a statement issued in Beirut on 25 November 1979 by the Arab Socialist Labor Party in the Arabian Peninsula, published as a document in "Opposition Forces in Saudi Arabia," *MERIP Reports,* February 1980, p. 16; and Jim Paul, "Insurrection at Mecca," *MERIP Reports,* October 1980, pp. 3–5.

33. Juhaiman al-'Utaibi, *Da'wah al-Ikhwan,* no. 3 (n.p.); see also Juhaiman al-'Utaibi, *Al-Imarah wa al-Bai'ah wa al-Ita'ah wa Kashf Talbis al-Hakkam 'ala Talabah al-'Ilm wa al-'Awam* (n.p.). For further information on political objectives of the rebels, see *The Neo-Ikhwan Seize the Grand Mosque in Mecca "Saudi Arabia"* (Denver: Saut al-Tali'ah, 1980), pp. 23–28; "Al-Amir Nayif Yukid Istimrar al-Muqawamah fi al-Saradib al-Muhajimun Istajaru' al-Khaliwat Qabl 6 Ash-hara wa Taddaribu' fi Haal Rimayah Qurb Jaddah," *Al-Nahar,* 1 December 1979; and Abuzar [pseud.], *Thawrah fi Rihab Makkah* (n.p., 1980).

34. "Ahdath al-Haram Bain al-Haqa'iq wa Abatil," *Saut al-Tali'ah* 6 (May 1980): 3–18.

35. Yousef Ibrahim, "New Data Link Mecca Takeover to Political Rift," *New York Times,* 25 February 1980.

36. "Les Forces Saoudiennes auraient repris contrôle total de la grande mosquée de la Mecque," *Le Monde,* 24 November 1979; *The Neo-Ikhwan Seize the Grand Mosque,* pp. 19–22.

Bibliography

Abuzar, [pseud.]. *Thawarh fi Rihab Makkah.* N.p., 1980.

"Ahdath al-Haram Bain al-Haqa'iq wa Abatil." *Saut al-Tali'ah* 6 (May 1980): 3–18.

Al-Awaji, Ibrahim. *Bureaucracy and Society in Saudi Arabia.* Ph.D. diss., University of Virginia, 1971.

Bacharach, Jere L. *A Near East Studies Handbook.* Rev. ed. Seattle: University of Washington Press, 1976.

Barker, Paul. *Saudi Arabia: The Development Dilemma.* London: Economist Intelligence Unit, 1982.

Ibn-Bayyan, Hayyan [pseud.]. "Poor Little Rich Nation, Open Letter to Saudi Arabia." *Nation.* 4 April 1981.

Birks, J. S., and C. A. Sinclair. *Arab Manpower, The Crisis of Development.* London: Croom Helm, 1980.

Braibanti, Ralph, and Fouad Abdul-Salam Al-Farsy. "Saudi Arabia: A Developmental Perspective." *Journal of South Asian and Middle Eastern Studies* 1 (September 1977): 3–43.

Burckhardt, John Lewis. *Notes on the Bedouins and Wahabys.* London: H. Colburn and R. Bentley, 1830.

Chamieh, Jebran, ed. *Saudi Arabia Yearbook, 1980–81.* Sin el Fil, Lebanon: The Research and Publishing House, 1980.

"Da'a'im al-Nizam al-Saudi." *Saut al-Tali'ah* 1 (April 1973): 5–17.

Dawisha, Adeed I. "Internal Values and External Threats: The Making of Saudi Foreign Policy." *Orbis* 23 (Spring 1979): 129–43.

———. "Saudi Arabia's Search for Security." *Adelphi Papers,* no. 158. London: International Institute for Strategic Studies, 1979–80.

Doughty, Charles. *Travels in Arabia Deserta.* New York: Liverright, 1926.

Economist Intelligence Unit. *Quarterly Economic Review of Saudi Arabia.* London: Economist Intelligence Unit, issues cited.

Edens, David G. "The Anatomy of the Saudi Revolution." *International Journal of Middle East Studies* 5 (1974): 50–64.

Al Farsy, Fouad A. *Saudi Arabia: A Case Study in Development.* London: Stacey International, 1978.

Fiches du Monde Arabe. *Arab World File.* "Saudi Arabia." Nicosia, Cyprus: various dates.

Ha'iat al-Amr bi al-Ma'ruf wa al-Nahi 'An al-Munkar." *Saut al-Tali'ah* 2 (April 1974): 10–30.

Halliday, Fred. *Arabia without Sultans: A Political Survey of Instability in the Arab World.* New York: Vintage Books, 1975.

Helms, Christine. *The Cohesion of Saudi Arabia: Evolution of Political Identity.* London: Croom Helm, 1981.

Hizb al-'Amal al-Ishtiraki al-'Arabi (Socialist Labor Party of Arabia). *Al-Wadh 'al-Tabaqi fi al-Jazirah al-'Arabiyah.* N.p.

Holden, David, and Richard Johns. *The House of Saud.* London: Pan Books, 1981.

Hottinger, Arnold. "The Rich Arab States in Trouble." *New York Review of Books.* 15 May 1980, pp. 23–24.

———. "Who Held the Grand Mosque Hostage?" *New York Review of Books.* 6 March 1980, pp. 35–36.

———. Human Rights in the Arabian Peninsula "Saudi Arabia." N.p.

International Institute for Strategic Studies. *The Military Balance.* London: International Institute for Strategic Studies, annual.

International Monetary Fund (IMF). *Balance of Payments Statistics.* Washington, D.C.: IMF, annual.

———. *International Financial Statistics.* Washington, D.C.: IMF, monthly.

Katakura, Motoko. *Bedouin Village, A Study of a Saudi Arabian People in Transition.* Tokyo: Tokyo University Press, 1977.

Khashoggi, Hani Yousef. *Local Adminstration in Saudi Arabia.* Ph.D. diss., Claremont University, 1979.

Kingdom of Saudi Arabia (K.O.S.A.), Central Planning Organization. *The First Development Plan 1390–1395 (1970–1975)*. Riyadh:
Central Planning Organization, 1970.
———, Industrial Studies and Development Center. *Industrial Struc-
ture and Development in Saudi Arabia*. Riyadh: Industrial Stud-
ies and Development Center, 1977.
———, Ministry of Finance and National Economy, Central Depart-
ment of Statistics. *Statistical Yearbook*. Riyadh: Central Depart-
ment of Statistics, annual.
———, *The Statistical Indicators*. Riyadh: Central Department of
Statistics, annual.
———, Ministry of Planning. *The Second Development Plan 1395–
1400 (1975–1980)*. Riyadh: Ministry of Planning, 1975.
———, *The Third Development Plan 1400–1405 (1980–1985)*. Riyadh:
Ministry of Planning, 1980.
———, Saudi Arabian Monetary Agency (SAMA). *Annual Report*.
Riyadh: SAMA, annual.
———. *Statistical Summary*. Riyadh: SAMA, annual.
Knauerhase, Ramon. "Saudi Arabia's Economy at the Beginning of
the 1970s." *Middle East Journal* 28 (Spring 1974): 126–40.
———. *The Saudi Arabian Economy*. New York: Praeger, 1975.
Kraft, Joseph. "Letter from Saudi Arabia." *The New Yorker*. 20
October 1975, pp. 111–39.
Labid [pseud.]. "Al-Ikhwan." *Saut al-Tali'ah* 1 (June 1973): 8–39.
Lacey, Robert. *The Kingdom*. New York: Harcourt Brace Jovanovich,
1982.
Lackner, Helen. *A House Built on Sand: A Political Economy of Saudi
Arabia*. London: Ithaca Press, 1978.
Looney, Robert. *Saudi Arabia's Development Potential*. Lexington,
Mass.: Lexington Books, 1982.
McGregor, R. "Saudi Arabia: Population and the Making of a Mod-
ern State." In *Populations of the Middle East and North Africa*,
edited by J. I. Clarke and W. B. Fisher, pp. 220–41. New York:
Africana Publishing Corporation, 1972.
El Mallakh, Ragaei. *Saudi Arabia, Rush to Development*. London:
Croom Helm, 1982.
El Mallakh, Ragaei, and Dorothea H. El Mallakh, eds. *Saudi Arabia:
Energy, Developmental Planning, and Industrialization*. Lexing-
ton, Mass.: Lexington Books, 1982.
"Al-Mamlikah al-'Arabiyah al-Sa'udiah, Wizarah al-'Adl." *Nizam al-
Qadha*. Riyadh, 1975.

Moliver, Donald M., and Paul J. Abbondante. *The Economy of Saudi Arabia.* New York: Praeger, 1980.

Munazammah al-Thawrah al-Islamiyah fi al-Jazirah al-'Arabiyah, *Intifazah al Haram.* 1981.

Murshid, Talal Asad. *Saudi Arabia: Administrative Aspects of Development.* Ph.D. diss., Claremont University, 1978.

The Neo-Ikhwan Seize the Grand Mosque in Mecca, "Saudi Arabia." Denver: Saut al-Tali'ah, 1980.

Niblock, Tim, ed. *Social and Economic Development in the Arab Gulf.* London: Croom Helm, 1980.

————. *State, Society and Economy in Saudi Arabia.* London: Croom Helm, 1982.

Nielsen, John; Paul Martin; Jane Whitmore; Chris Harper; and Tessa Namuth. "Saudi Arabia: A Shaky U.S. Pillar of Security." *Newsweek.* 3 March 1980, pp. 34–38.

Nyrop, Richard; Beryl Lieff Benderly; Loraine Newhouse Carter; Darrel R. Elgin; and Robert A. Kirchner. *Area Handbook for Saudi Arabia.* 3d. ed. Washington, D.C.: GPO, 1977.

"Opposition Forces in Saudi Arabia." *MERIP Reports.* February 1980, pp. 16–17.

Palgrave, William. *Narratives of a Year's Journey Through Central and Eastern Arabia, 1862–1863.* London: Macmillan and Co., 1866.

Paul, Jim. "Insurrection at Mecca." *MERIP Reports.* October 1980, pp. 3–5.

Philby, H. St. John. *Empty Quarter.* London: Constable, 1933.

————. *Arabian Days.* London: Robert Hale, 1948.

————. *Arabian Jubilee.* London: Robert Hale, 1952.

————. "The Scandal of Arabia." *London Sunday Times.* 23 and 30 October 1955.

"Al-Qatif." *Saut al-Tali'ah* 22 (May 1980): 190–211.

Quandt, William B. *Saudi Arabia in the 1980s.* Washington, D.C.: Brookings Institution, 1981.

"Al-Quwat al-Mussallahah." *Saut al-Tali'ah* 2 (January 1974): 8–34.

Rashid, Ahmid. *Al-Idarah al-Mahalliyah fi al-Mamlikah al-'Arabiyah al-Sa'udiah.* Cairo: Dar al-Sharq, 1981.

Al-Rawaf, Othman Yasin. *The Concept of Five Crises in Political Development—Relevance to the Kingdom of Saudi Arabia.* Ph.D. diss., Duke University, 1980.

Rugh, William. "The Emergence of a New Middle Class in Saudi Arabia." *Middle East Journal* 27 (Winter 1973): 7–20.

Al-Sabbab, Ahmad. *Al-Takhtit wa al-Tanmihah al-Iqtisadiyah fi al-Mamlikah al-'Arabiyah al-'Sa'udiyah.* Jidda, 1978.

"Sacrilege in Mecca." *Time.* 3 December 1979, pp. 50–51.

Al-Sa'id, Nasir. *Tarikh Al-i Sa'ud.* Beirut, 1979.

Salah [pseud.]. "Al-Mu'aridah al-Siyasiyah fi al-Sa'udiyah." *Saut al-Tali'ah* 1 (March 1973): 18–29.

Saudi Business and Arab Economic Report. Issues cited.

Shaw, John A., and David E. Long. *Saudi Arabian Modernization.* New York: Praeger, 1982.

Sheehan, Edward R. F. "The Epidemic of Money." *New York Times Magazine.* 14 November 1976.

Shilling, Nancy A. *Doing Business in Saudi Arabia and the Arab Gulf States.* New York: Inter-Crescent Publishing and Information Corporation, 1979.

Solaim, Soliman A. *Constitutional and Judicial Organization in Saudi Arabia.* Ph.D. diss., Johns Hopkins University, 1970.

Stockholm International Peace Research Institute. *World Armaments and Disarmament, SIPRI Yearbook 1978.* Cambridge, Mass., MIT Press, 1978.

Strasser, Steven; Paul Martin; William Schimdt; and Fred Coleman. "The Khomeini Contagion." *Newsweek.* 17 December 1979, pp. 39–40.

Al-'Utaibi, Juhaiman. *Da'wah al-Ikhwan,* no. 3. N.p.

———. *Al-Imarah wa al-Bai'ah wa al-Ita'ah wa Kashf Tablis al-Hukkam 'ala Talabah al-'Ilm wa al-'Awam.* N.p.

United Nations (U.N.). *Demographic Yearbook.* New York: U.N., annual.

———. *Yearbook of International Trade Statistics.* New York; U.N., annual.

———, Conference on Trade and Development. *Handbook of International Trade and Development Statistics.* New York: U.N., annual.

———, Economic Commission for Western Asia. *The Population Situation in the ECWA Region, Saudi Arabia.* Beirut: U.N. Economic Commission for Western Asia, 1979.

———, Educational, Scientific and Cultural Organization (UNESCO). *Statistical Yearbook.* Paris: UNESCO, annual.

U.S. Congress, House Committee on Foreign Affairs. Hearings. 29 July 1975.

———. *United States Arms Policies in the Persian Gulf and Red Sea Areas.* 95th Cong., 1st sess. Washington, D.C.: GPO, 1977.

———, Subcommittee on Europe and the Middle East. *Saudi Arabia and United States: The New Context in an Evolving "Special Relationship."* Report prepared by the Foreign Affairs and National Defense Division, Congressional Research Service, Library of Congress. 97th Cong., 1st sess. Washington, D.C.: GPO, 1981.

U.S. Congress, Senate Committee on Foreign Relations. *The Sale of F-15s to Saudi Arabia.* Report prepared by Hans Binnendijk and Bill Richardson. 95th Cong., 2d sess. Washington, D.C.: GPO, 1978.

———. Hearings. 3–5 May 1978.

———, Subcommittee on Multinationals. Hearings. 13, 30 May; 9, 10, 13 June; 29 July; 11 September 1975; and 7 April; 4 May 1976.

U.S. Department of State, Division of Research for Near East, South Asia, and Africa. *Saudi Arabia: A Disruptive Force in Western Arabia.* Intelligence report, no. 7144. 16 January 1956.

Wahba, Hafiz. *Arabian Days.* London: Arthur Baker, 1965.

Walpole, Norman C. et al. *Area Handbook for Saudi Arabia.* Washington, D.C.: GPO, 1977.

Wells, Donald A. *Saudi Arabian Development Strategy.* Washington, D.C.: American Enterprise Institute for Public Policy Research, 1976.

World Bank. *World Development Report.* New York: Oxford University Press, 1982.

———. *World Tables 1980.* Baltimore: Johns Hopkins University Press, 1980.

A. REZA S. ISLAMI is assistant professor of political science at the University of Washington. He has taught Middle East politics at Claremont University, Oxford; and at the University of California, Riverside.

Dr. Islami received his Ph.D. from UCLA and has been involved in research, as well as policy planning on the governmental level in the Middle East. He has written articles on administration, the military, religion, and revolution in the Middle East.

ROSTAM MEHRABAN KAVOUSSI is assistant professor in the Henry M. Jackson School of International Studies at the University of Washington. He has taught at the Iran Center for Management Studies, and the University of Pennsylvania.

Dr. Kavoussi received his Ph.D. in economics from Harvard. He is a specialist on economic development of the Middle East and international political economy. His research interests include the effects of oil exports on Middle Eastern economies and societies, and the role of international trade in economic development.

This monograph was set in Computer Modern fonts, using Donald Knuth's TeX typesetting system. The monograph format was written by Pierre MacKay, to editorial specifications established by Felicia Hecker, who also did most of the preparation of source files. The generous cooperation of the University of Washington Department of Computer Science is gratefully acknowledged. For further information about TeX, see the *TeXbook* by Donald Knuth (Addison-Wesley, 1984). It is hoped that the success of this monograph will inspire future authors to make their manuscripts available in computer readable form, using TeX.

TeX is a trademark of the American Mathematical Society.

Islami, A. Reza S.
    The political economy of Saudi Arabia.

    (Near Eastern studies / University of Washington :
no. 1)
    Bibliography: p.
    1. Saudi Arabia—Economic policy. 2. Saudi Arabia—
Social policy. 3. Saudi Arabia—Politics and government.
4. Petroleum industry and trade—Government policy—
Saudi Arabia. I. Kavoussi, Rostam Mehraban. II. Title.
III. Series: Near Eastern studies (Seattle, Wash.) ; no. 1.
HC415.33.I84   1984   338.953'8   83-26043
ISBN 0-295-96139-2